1982

$4-

THE TASTE OF
PASTA

Antonio Piccinardi

THE TASTE OF
PASTA

Webb & Bower

MICHAEL JOSEPH

Published in 1987 by
Webb & Bower (Publishers) Limited
9 Colleton Crescent, Exeter, Devon EX2 4BY
in association with Michael Joseph Limited
27 Wright's Lane, London W8 5TZ

Photographs: Emilio Fabio Simion
Drawings: Ezio Giglioli

The author would like to thank Laura Raffo
for her kind assistance.

Translated from the Italian by Elaine Hardy
Copyright © 1986 Arnoldo Mondadori Editore
S.p.A., Milan
Copyright © 1987 Arnoldo Mondadori Editore
S.p.A., Milan for the English translation

British Library Cataloguing in Publication Data
Piccinardi, Antonio
  Taste of pasta.
  1. Cookery (Macaroni)
  I. Title II. Il gusto della pasta. *English*
  641.8′22   TX809.M17

ISBN 0-86350-174-5

Printed and bound in Italy by Arnoldo Mondadori
Editore, Verona.

Contents

Laur + Robt ✓

Foreword

'… in a country called Bengodi, where the vines are tied up with sausages … there was a mountain all of grated Parmesan cheese, whereon abode folk who did nothing but make macaroni and ravioli and cook them in capon-broth, after which they threw them down thence and whoso got most thereof had most …'
(Giovanni Boccaccio, *The Decameron*)

Pasta is one of the most versatile and flexible of foods, marrying perfectly with fish, shellfish, meat, eggs, cheese and vegetables. Basic recipes can be used time and time again, adapted to suit any occasion, providing infinite scope for the creative cook.

The origins of pasta are lost in the mists of time: it was certainly known and used centuries ago in the East as well as in Italy, and the earliest pictorial references to pasta can be seen in frescoes decorating the walls of Etruscan tombs. In Book IV of his *De arte coquinaria*, the famous Roman gastronome Apicius writes about 'lagana', a type of pasta very similar to the lasagna used today. 'Lasagna' is also mentioned in a thirteenth-century manuscript now kept in the library at the University of Bologna. Such documents provide further evidence in support of the theory that, contrary to popular belief, pasta was not introduced to Europe by Marco Polo on his return from China.

The recipes in this collection are for the most part Mediterranean in origin, but the ingredients used are universally available in Italian stores and delicatessens.

The recipes selected and the cooking methods used to prepare them are those of traditional Italian cookery, but combine the innovations of modern cuisine with simplicity of preparation. All recipes serve four but the ingredients can be increased proportionally for extra servings. Preparation times take into account the time required for making fresh pasta, the filling and the sauce.

This volume also contains useful information on all aspects of cooking pasta, including how to prepare fresh pasta at home, basic sauce recipes, which utensils to use, the names of the many types of fresh and dried pasta and a short but essential glossary.

Buon appetito!

Silverware, cutlery, china, saucepans and table linen for the photographs were kindly loaned by: Accornero, Basile, Ceragioli, Colle, Corradi, Farmache, Laboratorio Pesaro, Medagliani, Morone, Pomellato, R.C.R., Richard-Ginori, Rosenthal-Thomas-Classic Rose, Rovere, Sambonet, Schönhuber-Franchi, Sebring. Particular thanks are extended to the Messulam Co., and to the chef Fabio Zago who tested the recipes.

Note

Both metric and imperial measurements are given. Use one or other system but do not mix the two, since conversions are working approximations.

The best flour to use for making fresh pasta is durum wheat, known in Italian as 'tipo OO'. This is available from Italian delicatessens. Perfectly good results are obtained, however, by using plain flour. Unless otherwise stated, plain or strong white flour can be used for all the recipes in this book.

Pasta with meat

Pasta bows with venison sauce

Preparation: 1½ hours (+8 hours for marinating)

225 g/8 oz pasta bows
225 g/8 oz venison (leg)
½ onion
½ carrot
1 stick celery
225 ml/8 fl oz red wine

1 bay leaf
2 sage leaves
50 g/2 oz butter
3 tbsp olive oil
salt
black pepper
½ sweet red pepper

1 Cut the venison into 2-cm/¾-in cubes. Dice the onion and carrot and cut the celery into small pieces.

2 Marinate the venison for 8 hours with the chopped vegetables, wine, bay leaf and sage.

3 Strain the marinade and reserve the liquid. Heat half the butter and 1 tbsp olive oil in a saucepan and add the meat and vegetables. Fry gently for 5 minutes. Season with salt and freshly ground black pepper.

4 Pour in the reserved marinade and simmer gently for 40 minutes until reduced.

5 Cut the pepper into thin strips, and fry gently in the remaining oil and butter for 10 minutes. Sprinkle with salt and add to the meat.

6 Cook the pasta bows in boiling salted water for 10–12 minutes or until *al dente*. Drain and pour into a saucepan with the venison sauce. Stir well and serve in heated dishes.

Suggested wines

Santa Maddalena, Chianti (Italy); Côtes de Provence Rosé (France); Californian Blanc de Noirs (U.S.A.); Rhine Sylvaner (Germany).

Agnolotti in rich meat sauce

Preparation: 2 hours

600 g/1¼ lb agnolotti
6 tbsp roast meat juices

For the pasta
225 g/8 oz flour
2 eggs
1 egg yolk
salt

For the filling
125 g/4 oz chicory
175 g/6 oz roast veal
125 g/4 oz braised beef
1 egg
50 g/2 oz grated Parmesan
4 tbsp braising liquor
salt
black pepper
nutmeg

1 Rinse and blanch the chicory.

2 Finely chop the veal and beef.

3 Mix together in a bowl the blanched and chopped chicory, the chopped meats, the egg, Parmesan and 4 tbsp braising liquor.

4 Stir the ingredients well, season with salt and freshly ground black pepper and add a pinch of grated nutmeg.

5 Shape the mixture into small balls. Roll out half the prepared pasta dough (p. 180) and place the filling at regular intervals on top. Cover with the remaining dough, press well around the filling to seal and cut into squares with a pastry wheel.

6 Cook the agnolotti in salted boiling water or stock for 3 minutes, then drain well.

7 Heat the roast meat juices in a frying pan and stir well.

8 Add the drained agnolotti and mix gently before serving.

Suggested wines

Dolcetto di Diano d'Alba, Valpolicella (Italy); Beaujolais (France); Californian Blanc de Noirs (U.S.A.); Moselle Riesling (Germany).

Saffron spaghetti

Preparation: 20 minutes

275 g/10 oz spaghetti
50 g/2 oz butter
salt

½ tsp saffron threads or 1
  envelope
125 ml/4 fl oz single cream
1 tbsp meat juices
40 g/1½ oz grated Parmesan
black pepper

1 Break the spaghetti into pieces.

2 Place the spaghetti in a saucepan with half the butter, two ladles of boiling water and a pinch of salt and simmer, stirring occasionally.

3 Check the pasta as it cooks, stirring occasionally and gradually adding a little more boiling water as the water in the pan evaporates.

4 Soak the saffron threads in a little warm water and add to the spaghetti after 5 minutes.

5 Just before the spaghetti is cooked, after 10–12 minutes, stir in the cream, the remaining butter, 1 tbsp meat juices and finally the Parmesan.

6 Mix well, stirring vigorously and sprinkle with freshly ground black pepper before serving in heated dishes.

Suggested wines

Pinot Champenois dell'Oltrepò Pavese, Greco di Tufo (Italy); Pouilly Fumé (France); Californian Chardonnay (U.S.A.); Moselle Riesling (Germany).

Penne with kidneys

Preparation: 50 minutes

250 g/9 oz penne
225 g/8 oz veal kidney
50 g/2 oz butter
1 clove garlic
salt
1 tbsp chopped fresh parsley
black pepper

1 Cut away the fat surrounding the kidney. Remove the membrane and cut out the hard core. Cut in half and soak in cold water for 10 minutes. Rinse and dry the kidney and cut into small pieces.

2 Melt the butter in a large frying pan; add the crushed garlic and chopped kidney, season with salt and cook over moderate heat for 6–7 minutes.

3 Meanwhile, cook the penne in boiling salted water for 10–12 minutes until *al dente*, then drain.

4 Pour the penne into the frying pan. Sprinkle with chopped parsley and freshly ground black pepper. Stir well before serving.

Suggested wines

Lagrein Rosato dell'Alto Adige, Valpolicella (Italy); Rosé d'Anjou (France); Californian Blanc de Noirs (U.S.A.); Blanc Fumé (South Africa).

Fettuccine with prosciutto and cream cheese

Preparation: 20 minutes

350 g/12 oz fettuccine
salt
125 g/4 oz cooked prosciutto, in
  one slice
125 g/4 oz mascarpone (cream
  cheese)
2–3 tbsp grated Parmesan
black pepper

1 Cook the fettuccine in boiling salted water for 6 minutes until *al dente*. Drain.

2 Cut the prosciutto into thin strips. Heat for a few minutes in a saucepan with 1 tbsp cream cheese.

3 Mix together the remaining cream cheese, Parmesan and a little freshly ground black pepper in a warm serving dish and stir well.

4 Add the piping hot fettuccine and the strips of prosciutto. Stir well and serve.

Suggested wines

Soave, Frascati (Italy); Bourgogne Blanc (France); Californian Pinot Blanc (U.S.A.), Moselle Riesling (Germany).

Tortellini in rich tomato sauce

Preparation: 2 hours

600 g/1¼ lb tortellini
300 g/10 oz skinned
   tomatoes
1 sprig rosemary
4 fresh basil leaves
salt
225 ml/8 fl oz single cream

For the pasta
225 g/8 oz flour
2 eggs
1 egg yolk
salt

For the filling
25 g/1 oz butter

125 g/4 oz pork sausage
50 g/2 oz turkey breast
salt
50 g/2 oz prosciutto
50 g/2 oz mortadella
1 egg
black pepper
nutmeg
100 g/3½ oz grated Parmesan
2 litres/3½ pints chicken stock

Suggested wines

Rosato del Salento, Lambrusco di Sorbara (Italy); Rosé de Loire (France); Californian Johannisberg Riesling (U.S.A.); Sauvignon Blanc (New Zealand).

1 Melt the butter in a frying pan and add the diced pork sausage and turkey breast. Sprinkle with salt and cook for 15 minutes.

2 Leave to cool slightly then chop finely with the prosciutto and mortadella.

3 Beat the egg with a pinch of salt, freshly ground black pepper and nutmeg and mix with the chopped meats in a bowl. Stir in the Parmesan and mix well.

4 Roll out the prepared pasta dough (p. 180) and cut into 5-cm/2-in squares.

5 Place a ball of filling in the centre of each square of pasta, fold in half to make a triangle and press the edges firmly to seal.

6 Join the two side points and press together, then fold over the third point towards the middle.

7 Bring the stock or salted water to the boil and cook the tortellini for about 4 minutes. Drain.

8 Meanwhile, prepare the tomato sauce. Purée the skinned tomatoes in a blender. Place in a frying pan with the rosemary, basil and a pinch of salt and cook for 8 minutes. Discard the rosemary and basil. Stir in the cream and heat until the sauce is slightly reduced. Pour the tortellini into the pan and heat for 1 minute before serving.

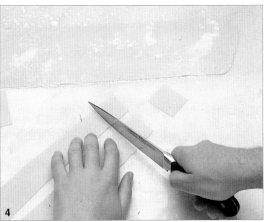

Macaroni with oxtail and sweet peppers

Preparation: 3 hours

250 g/9 oz macaroni
450 g/1 lb oxtail
salt
4 tbsp olive oil
½ small onion, cut into thin
  strips
1 large sweet yellow pepper

½ sweet red pepper
3 tbsp freshly made tomato
  sauce
2 tbsp grated Parmesan
black pepper

1 Simmer the oxtail in boiling salted water in a covered saucepan for about 2 hours. Drain, reserving the stock, and leave to cool slightly.

2 Pour the olive oil into a frying pan. Cut the onions and sweet peppers into 4-cm/1½-in squares and add them to the frying pan; sprinkle with salt and cook for 4 minutes. Add the tomato sauce and cook for a few more minutes until the peppers have softened a little.

3 Remove the meat from the oxtail and break into pieces.

4 Add the meat to the peppers, pour over a little of the reserved stock and heat gently for about 6 minutes.

5 Cook the macaroni in plenty of boiling salted water for 10–12 minutes or until *al dente*. Drain.

6 Pour the macaroni into the saucepan containing the sauce. Sprinkle with Parmesan and freshly ground black pepper. Stir well and serve.

Suggested wines

Lago di Caldaro, Chianti (Italy); Rosé de Loire (France); Californian Sauvignon Blanc (U.S.A.); Rhine Riesling (Germany).

Sardinian gnocchetti with sausage ragoût

Preparation: 40 minutes

250 g/9 oz Sardinian gnocchetti
175 g/6 oz spicy sausage
2 tbsp olive oil
½ onion
1 clove garlic
2 fresh basil leaves

350 g/12 oz ripe tomatoes
salt
black pepper
1 tbsp wild fennel leaves
50 g/2 oz grated Sardinian
    Pecorino cheese

1 Slice the sausage and place in a saucepan with the olive oil, the chopped onion, garlic and basil.

2 Heat for a few minutes then add the skinned, seeded and chopped tomatoes. Season with salt and freshly ground black pepper and heat gently for 15 minutes. Remove the garlic and basil and add the chopped fennel leaves.

3 Cook the gnocchetti in plenty of boiling salted water for 2–3 minutes or until *al dente*.

4 Mix with the sausage and tomato sauce and sprinkle with the grated Pecorino cheese.

Suggested wines

Torbato, Corvo di Salaparuta (Italy); Bâtard Montrachet (France); Californian Gewürztraminer (U.S.A.); Rhine Riesling (Germany).

Maltagliati with duck

Preparation: 2 hours

350 g/12 oz maltagliati
1 young duck, cleaned, liver
 reserved
3 carrots
1 onion
1 stick celery
1 tbsp chopped fresh parsley

400 ml/14 fl oz red wine
salt
black pepper
125 g/4 oz courgettes
1 tbsp olive oil
50 g/2 oz butter
16 black olives, pitted

For the pasta
225 g/8 oz flour
2 eggs
1 egg yolk
salt

Suggested wines

Santa Maddalena, Bardolino Chiaretto (Italy); Beaujolais
(France); Californian Pinot Noir (U.S.A.); Cabernet (South
Africa).

1 Prepare the pasta dough (p. 180) by mixing together the flour, eggs, salt and a little water. Roll out in a thin sheet and cut into rectangles, then triangles, using a sharp knife.

2 Using a sharp knife, carefully cut away the breast fillets from the duck.

3 Roughly chop the rest of the carcass into pieces and place in a saucepan with one carrot, the onion, celery and chopped parsley. Add the red wine and simmer for about 15 minutes until slightly reduced.

4 Strain the stock and adjust the seasoning. Add the crushed reserved duck liver and cook for a few more minutes.

5 Cut the courgettes and remaining carrots into thin strips and blanch in boiling salted water for a couple of minutes.

6 Brown the duck breast fillets briefly in the olive oil; sprinkle with salt and pepper and cook for a few minutes so that the meat is still pink.

7 Leave to cool slightly then cut into small pieces.

8 Cook the maltagliati in boiling salted water for 2–3 minutes only, then drain. Put the sauce, butter, vegetables, sliced duck, halved olives and drained maltagliati into a large frying pan. Season with salt and pepper and stir well before serving.

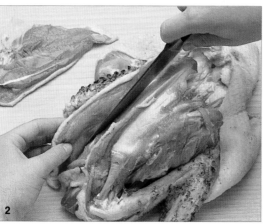

Macaroni with meat sauce

Preparation: 2 hours

250 g/9 oz fluted macaroni
40 g/1½ oz butter
250 g/9 oz ground beef

50 g/2 oz spicy sausage
1 bay leaf
½ onion
1 clove
salt
225 g/8 oz tomatoes
a little stock
4 tbsp grated Parmesan
black pepper

1 Melt half the butter in a saucepan. Add the ground beef, chopped sausage, bay leaf and the onion (left whole, stuck with the clove) and brown gently for 20 minutes.

2 Season with salt. Skin and chop the tomatoes, stir into the meat and simmer for about 1 hour, adding a little stock if necessary. After an hour discard the onion and bay leaf.

3 Cook the macaroni in plenty of boiling salted water for 10–12 minutes or until *al dente*. Drain.

4 Pour the macaroni into a large heated tureen. Add the remaining butter, the meat sauce, grated Parmesan and a sprinkling of freshly ground black pepper. Stir well and serve.

Suggested wines

Bardolino Chiaretto, Valpolicella (Italy); Côtes du Rhône (France); Californian Gewürztraminer (U.S.A.); Müller Thurgau (Germany).

Agnolotti poacher's style

Preparation: 2 hours

600 g/1¼ lb agnolotti
50 g/2 oz butter
4 sage leaves
2–3 tbsp grated Parmesan

For the pasta
225 g/8 oz flour
2 eggs

1 egg yolk, salt

For the filling
225 g/8 oz lettuce
50 g/2 oz butter
½ clove garlic
1 tbsp chopped onion
1 tbsp olive oil
350 g/12 oz mixed game
    (pheasant, rabbit, duck)

salt
150 ml/5 fl oz white wine
1 egg
25 g/1 oz grated Parmesan
nutmeg
black pepper

1 Rinse the lettuce and blanch in salted water. Drain and chop.

2 Melt 50 g/2 oz butter in a frying pan. Add the finely chopped garlic, onion and lettuce and fry over moderate heat for 5 minutes.

3 Pour the olive oil into another frying pan. Add the game, cut into pieces, season with salt, pour in the wine and simmer for 20 minutes. Strain, then chop the meat. Place in a bowl with the fried onion and lettuce mixture, the beaten egg, 25 g/1 oz grated Parmesan, a pinch of nutmeg,

salt and pepper. Stir well and shape into small balls. Roll out half the prepared pasta dough (p. 180) and place balls of filling at regular intervals on top.

4 Cover with the remaining dough; press well all around the filling to seal and cut into squares with a pastry wheel.

5 Melt the remaining 50 g/2 oz butter and heat the sage leaves for a few minutes. Cook the agnolotti in boiling salted water for 3 minutes. Drain well, sprinkle with grated Parmesan and cover with the sage butter.

Suggested wines

Valpolicella, Dolcetto di Diano d'Alba (Italy); Rosé de Loire (France); Californian Blanc de Noirs (U.S.A.); Müller Thurgau (Germany).

Pappardelle with partridge

Preparation: 1 hour 40 minutes (+6 hours for the pasta to dry)

350 g/12 oz pappardelle
2 partridges
2 slices streaky bacon
2 sprigs rosemary
50 g/2 oz butter

1 tbsp olive oil
salt
black pepper
4 juniper berries
25 g/1 oz onion
½ stick celery
150 ml/5 fl oz white wine
50 g/2 oz truffle

For the pasta
225 g/8 oz flour
2 eggs
1 egg yolk
salt

Suggested wines

Lago di Caldaro, Dolcetto di Diano d'Alba (Italy); Côtes du Rhône Rosé (France); Californian Gewürztraminer (U.S.A.); Rhine Sylvaner (Germany).

1 Prepare the pasta dough (p. 180) by mixing together the flour, eggs and a pinch of salt. Roll into a thin sheet, cut into 2-cm/¾-in-wide strips and leave to dry for at least 6 hours.

2 Clean, singe and rinse the partridges. Pat dry with kitchen paper.

3 Wrap a slice of bacon round each sprig of rosemary and place one inside each partridge.

4 Heat the butter and olive oil in a saucepan and brown the partridges on all sides. Season with salt and freshly ground black pepper.

5 Add the juniper berries, the chopped onion and celery and pour in the wine. As the wine evaporates add a few tablespoons of hot water or stock.

6 When the partridges are cooked, remove all the meat and tear into pieces. Keep the meat hot.

7 Break the carcasses with a cleaver and place in a saucepan with the cooking juices. Add 4 tbsp hot water and cook for 10 minutes. Strain through a fine sieve, reserving the stock.

8 Cook the pappardelle in boiling salted water for 4 minutes until *al dente*. Drain, then put in a saucepan with the reserved stock and meat. Stir well. Serve in individual dishes and sprinkle with slivers of truffle, thinly sliced with a mandoline cutter.

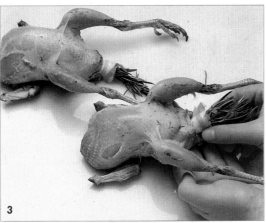

Penne scarlatte

Preparation: 30 minutes

275 g/10 oz penne
125 g/4 oz cooked tongue
50 g/2 oz butter

5 tbsp meat juices
4 tbsp white sauce
2 tbsp grated Parmesan
salt
white pepper

1 Cut the tongue into thin strips.

2 Place the butter, meat juices, white sauce (p. 32) and the Parmesan in a large saucepan. Heat over another saucepan of boiling water, beating with a whisk, until the sauce is smooth.

3 Meanwhile, cook the penne in boiling salted water for 10–12 minutes until *al dente*. Drain.

4 Pour the penne into the pan containing the sauce. Add pepper and heat for 1 minute.

5 Serve the penne in individual heated dishes, sprinkle with the strips of tongue and serve immediately.

Suggested wines

Pinot Bianco del Collio, Pinot Champenois di Franciacorta (Italy); Pouligny Montrachet (France); Californian Chenin Blanc (U.S.A.); Rhine Sylvaner (Germany).

Spaghetti alla carbonara

Preparation: 30 minutes

275 g/10 oz spaghetti
125 g/4 oz pancetta or bacon
1 tbsp olive oil
1 clove garlic
2 eggs

salt
black pepper
2 tbsp grated Pecorino cheese
2 tbsp grated Parmesan

1 Cut the bacon into small dice.

2 Heat the olive oil in a small saucepan, add the crushed garlic and bacon and brown gently for 3 minutes. Discard the garlic.

3 Cook the spaghetti in boiling salted water for 10–12 minutes until *al dente*. Drain.

4 Beat together the eggs, salt, freshly ground black pepper and grated cheeses and pour into a very hot tureen.

5 Pour the spaghetti into the tureen.

6 Add the browned bacon and any remaining oil. Stir well before serving.

Suggested wines

Rosato del Salento, Bardolino Chiaretto (Italy); Rosé d'Anjou (France); Californian Chardonnay (U.S.A.); Moselle Riesling (Germany).

Duck ravioli with pepper sauce

Preparation: 1 hour

600 g/1¼ lb ravioli
3 tbsp single cream
80 g/3 oz butter
3 tbsp creamed pepper sauce
   (p. 178)

For the pasta
200 g/7 oz flour
2 eggs
salt

For the filling
275 g/10 oz duck breast,
   skinned
50 g/2 oz spinach
2 tbsp fresh breadcrumbs

150 ml/5 fl oz milk
15 g/½ oz butter
2 shallots
25 g/1 oz mushrooms
25 g/1 oz bone marrow,
   chopped
2 tbsp chopped fresh parsley
50 ml/2 fl oz single cream
salt
black pepper

Suggested wines

Sauvignon del Collio, Terlano dell'Alto Adige (Italy); Bâtard Montrachet (France); Californian Johannisberg Riesling (U.S.A.); Rhine Sylvaner (Germany).

1 Finely chop the duck breast.

2 Cook the spinach in boiling water for 5–7 minutes until tender.

3 Soak the breadcrumbs in the milk. Squeeze out excess liquid and add to the spinach.

4 Melt 15 g/½ oz butter and brown the chopped shallots and the mushrooms. Add the chopped duck breast and cook for another 5 minutes, stirring frequently.

5 Remove from the heat, add the spinach, bone marrow, chopped parsley and cream. Stir, season with salt and pepper and cook for 3–4 minutes.

6 Roll out half the prepared pasta dough (p. 180). Place little balls of filling at regular intervals on the dough and cover with the remaining sheet of dough. Press well all around the filling to seal and cut into squares with a pastry wheel.

7 Cook the ravioli in boiling salted water for 5 minutes. Drain well. Pour 3 tbsp cream into a frying pan; stir in 80 g/3 oz butter over moderate heat and beat with a whisk until slightly reduced.

8 Stir in the creamed pepper sauce and mix well. Add the ravioli and stir gently to coat with the sauce before serving.

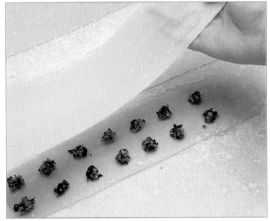

Country-style macaroni

Preparation: 1 hour

250 g/9 oz fluted macaroni
3 artichokes
1 lemon
4 tbsp olive oil
2 tbsp chopped onion
125 g/4 oz spicy Italian sausage

½ red chilli pepper
4 tbsp white wine
salt
2 tbsp grated Parmesan
black pepper

1 Trim the artichokes: pull off any hard outer leaves and trim the sharp tips with scissors.

2 Cut the artichokes in half, cut out and discard the hairy choke. Slice the artichokes finely lengthwise. Leave to soak in water acidulated with the juice of the lemon.

3 Pour the olive oil into a large saucepan and gently fry the chopped onion for 2 minutes. Add the drained and dried artichokes; stir and cook for 5 minutes.

4 Skin the sausage and crumble into pieces. Sprinkle over the artichokes and add the finely chopped chilli pepper.

5 Add the white wine and cook for a further 5 minutes, stirring well. Add a few tablespoons of boiling water and mix well.

6 Cook the macaroni in boiling salted water for 10–12 minutes or until *al dente*.

7 Pour the pasta into the pan containing the sauce. Sprinkle with Parmesan, add freshly ground black pepper and stir well over high heat for 1 minute. Serve in heated dishes.

Suggested wines

Lagrein Rosato dell'Alto Adige, Grignolino del Monferrato Casalese (Italy); Beaujolais (France); Californian Blanc de Noirs (U.S.A.); Rhine Riesling (Germany).

Ravioli with guinea fowl and truffles

Preparation: 1 hour 40 minutes

600 g/1¼ lb ravioli
25 g/1 oz white truffle paste

For the pasta
225 g/8 oz flour
2 eggs
1 egg yolk
salt

For the filling
½ guinea fowl
50 g/2 oz butter
black pepper
125 ml/4 fl oz white wine
2 tbsp fresh breadcrumbs,
    soaked in milk
1 tbsp chopped fresh parsley,
    marjoram and chives
2 tbsp grated Parmesan

1 Cut the guinea fowl in half. Melt 40 g/1½ oz butter in a saucepan and brown the guinea fowl. Season with salt and pepper and pour in the wine. Cook for about 40 minutes, then leave to cool before boning. Reserve the cooking juices.

2 Chop the meat finely and place in a bowl with the breadcrumbs, the remaining butter, melted, the chopped herbs, Parmesan and a little freshly ground black pepper. Mix well.

3 Roll out half of the prepared pasta dough (p. 180) and place small balls of filling at regular intervals on top. Cover with the remaining dough; press firmly all around the filling to seal and cut into squares with a pastry wheel.

4 Cook the ravioli in plenty of boiling salted water for 5 minutes, then drain.

5 Strain the cooking juices from the guinea fowl through a fine sieve. Heat gently in a saucepan and stir in the truffle paste. Pour the ravioli into the saucepan, stir gently then serve in heated dishes.

Suggested wines

Lagrein Rosato dell'Alto Adige, Grignolino del Monferrato Casalese (Italy); Côtes de Provence Rosé (France); Californian Blanc de Noirs (U.S.A.); Chardonnay (South Africa).

Baked spinach lasagne

Preparation: 1 hour 20 minutes

250 g/9 oz spinach lasagne

For the meat sauce
25 g/1 oz pancetta
1 tbsp onion
½ carrot
½ stick celery
80 g/3 oz butter

125 g/4 oz pork sausage
125 g/4 oz beef
50 g/2 oz prosciutto
1 tbsp freshly made tomato
  sauce
50 g/2 oz chicken livers
2–3 tbsp single cream
black pepper
50 g/2 oz grated Parmesan

For the white sauce
40 g/1½ oz butter
40 g/1½ oz flour
500 ml/18 fl oz milk
salt
white pepper
For the pasta
225 g/8 oz flour
2 eggs, 1 egg yolk
225 g/8 oz cooked spinach

Suggested wines

Lambrusco di Sorbara, Bardolino Chiaretto (Italy); Côtes de Provence Rosé (France); Californian Gewürztraminer (U.S.A.); Rhine Riesling (Germany).

1 Finely chop the pancetta, onion, carrot and celery.

2 Brown gently in 40 g/1½ oz butter, then add the minced pork sausage, beef and prosciutto.

3 Cook for another 3 minutes, then add the tomato sauce, diluted in a ladleful of hot water. Add salt and simmer gently for 40 minutes, adding more water if necessary.

4 Prepare the spinach lasagne (p. 181), combining the flour, eggs, a pinch of salt and the cooked and finely chopped spinach. Roll out and cut into wide strips, then into squares.

5 Cook the lasagne for 3–5 minutes in plenty of boiling salted water (add 1 tbsp olive oil to prevent the pasta from sticking together). When they are *al dente*, drain and rinse with cold water to prevent further cooking. Place in a single layer on a clean tea towel to dry.

6 Prepare the white sauce: melt the butter, add the flour and stir for 3 minutes. Stir in the hot milk gradually and cook for about 10 minutes. Season with salt and pepper. The sauce should be quite thick.

7 Cut the chicken livers into small pieces and add to the meat sauce. Cook for 3 minutes, then stir in the cream. Simmer for 4 minutes, adjust the seasoning and sprinkle with a little freshly ground black pepper.

8 Butter an ovenproof dish and place a layer of lasagne in the bottom. Sprinkle with a little grated Parmesan, then with meat sauce, followed by white sauce. Repeat the procedure, making a second layer, then finish with a layer of lasagne. Cover with a thin layer of white sauce, sprinkle with Parmesan and a few dots of butter. Bake in a preheated oven at 180°C/350°F/mark 4 for about 20 minutes.

33

Tagliolini with chicken livers

Preparation: 30 minutes

275 g/10 oz egg tagliolini
150 g/5 oz chicken livers
250 g/9 oz canned tomatoes
1 sprig rosemary
salt

pinch sugar
1 tbsp olive oil
40 g/1½ oz butter
2 fresh sage leaves
black pepper

1 Trim the fat from the livers.

2 Cut into 1-cm/½-in pieces. Rinse under running water for 1 minute then dry well.

3 Liquidize the tomatoes in a blender and cook in a small saucepan for 7 minutes with the rosemary, salt, sugar and 1 tbsp olive oil.

4 Melt the butter in a large saucepan. Stir in the sage and chicken livers and cook for 2–3 minutes over low heat.

5 Cook the tagliolini in boiling salted water for 6 minutes or until *al dente*. Drain well.

6 Remove the rosemary from the hot tomato sauce. Pour the sauce over the chicken livers.

7 Place the saucepan over moderate heat, add the tagliolini, season with pepper and stir well before serving.

Suggested wines

Pinot Grigio dell'Alto Adige, Tocai del Collio (Italy); Bordeaux Blanc (France); Chardonnay (Australia); Californian Pinot Blanc (U.S.A.).

Pappardelle with hare sauce

Preparation: 2 hours

350 g/12 oz pappardelle
1 small hare
1 onion
1 carrot
1 stick celery
6 tbsp olive oil
1 tbsp chopped fresh parsley
salt

black pepper
250 ml/9 fl oz red wine
150 ml/5 fl oz milk
6 tbsp grated Parmesan

For the pasta
225 g/8 oz flour
2 eggs
1 egg yolk
salt

1 Clean the hare, reserving the blood. Cut off the forelegs and head and reserve, together with the heart and liver. (Only the front half of the hare will be used.)

2 Chop the onion, carrot and celery. Heat the olive oil in a large saucepan, add the chopped vegetables and parsley. Add the reserved forelegs, head, heart and liver and season with salt and pepper. Brown over high heat for a few minutes. Pour in the wine, allow to evaporate then add the blood diluted in a little hot water. Cook for a few minutes more then pour in the milk. Simmer for a further 30 minutes. Strain the cooking liquor, reserving the meat and returning the sauce to the pan.

3 Cut away the meat from the forelegs and head and cut the heart and liver into small pieces. Add the pieces of meat to the sauce. Bring to the boil, then cook for a few more minutes.

4 Prepare the pappardelle (p. 181) and cook in boiling salted water for 4 minutes. Drain well. Top with the hare sauce and sprinkle with Parmesan.

Suggested wines

Chianti, Dolcetto di Diano d'Alba (Italy); Beaujolais (France); Californian Pinot Noir (U.S.A.); Cabernet (South Africa).

Bucatini all'amatriciana

Preparation: 30 minutes

325 g/12 oz bucatini
125 g/4 oz pancetta
275 g/10 oz ripe tomatoes
3 tbsp olive oil
salt
½ clove garlic
2 leaves fresh basil

½ red chilli pepper
3 tbsp grated Parmesan
3 tbsp grated mature Pecorino
  cheese

1 Cut the rind off the pancetta and cut into 5 mm × 4 cm/ ¼ × 1½ in strips.

2 Prepare the tomato sauce: skin, seed and coarsely chop the tomatoes. Heat in a frying pan for 10 minutes with the olive oil, a little salt and the garlic. Add the basil and cook for a further 5 minutes.

3 Remove the garlic and basil and sieve the tomatoes.

4 Gently brown the pancetta in no extra oil with the finely chopped chilli pepper.

5 Cook the bucatini in plenty of boiling salted water for 10–12 minutes until *al dente*. Drain.

6 Pour the bucatini into a heated serving dish. Sprinkle with the pancetta and any fat in the pan, the tomato sauce and grated cheeses. Stir, cover and leave to stand for 3 minutes before serving.

Suggested wines

Frascati, Torgiano Bianco (Italy); Bordeaux Blanc (France); Californian Pinot Blanc (U.S.A.); Müller Thurgau (Germany).

Genoese ravioli

Preparation: 2½ hours

600 g/1¼ lb ravioli
salt
6 tbsp roast meat juices
3 tbsp grated Parmesan

For the pasta
250 g/9 oz flour
water
salt

For the filling
225 g/8 oz Batavian endive
175 g/6 oz borage
salt

40 g/1½ oz butter
175 g/6 oz veal
50 g/2 oz calf's brains
50 g/2 oz veal sweetbreads
1 tbsp fresh breadcrumbs
2 eggs
1 tbsp fresh marjoram
3 tbsp grated Parmesan
black pepper

1 Trim and rinse the endive and borage. Cook in boiling salted water for 6 minutes. Drain.

2 Melt the butter in a saucepan and add the chopped veal. Brown and cook gently for about 20 minutes.

3 Rinse the brains and sweetbreads. Leave to soak in warm water for about 30 minutes. Remove the thin skin surrounding them. Simmer in plenty of boiling salted water for 15 minutes, then drain.

4 Grind the veal (reserving the cooking juices), brains, sweetbreads, endive and borage in a grinder or food processor until the mixture is smooth.

5 Spoon the mixture into a bowl and add the fresh breadcrumbs, moistened in the butter in which the veal was cooked.

6 Beat the eggs together with the finely chopped marjoram, grated Parmesan, salt and pepper. Add to the mixture in the bowl and stir well.

7 Roll out half the prepared pasta dough (p. 180). Shape the filling into small balls and place them at 4-cm/1½-in intervals on top of the sheet of dough. Cover with the remaining sheet of dough and press firmly all around the filling to seal. Cut into squares with a pastry wheel.

8 Cook the ravioli in boiling salted water for 5 minutes. Drain well. Turn into a heated serving dish and sprinkle with the hot roast meat juices and grated Parmesan.

Suggested wines

Tocai del Collio, Torgiano Bianco (Italy); Bordeaux Blanc (France); Californian Chardonnay (U.S.A.); Rhine Sylvaner (Germany).

Bucatini with duck sauce

Preparation: 2 hours

275 g/10 oz bucatini
1 young duck
1 carrot
½ onion
1 stick celery
salt
3 tbsp olive oil

25 g/1 oz butter
4 fresh sage leaves
black pepper
50 g/2 oz grated Parmesan

1 Clean, singe and rinse the duck. Reserve the liver.

2 Fill a large saucepan with cold water and add the carrot, onion, celery, the duck and a little salt.

3 Bring to the boil and simmer for about 1 hour or until the duck is tender. (Use the duck meat for another dish.)

4 Drain the duck stock into another saucepan and cook the bucatini in it for 10–12 minutes. Drain well.

5 Meanwhile, heat the olive oil and butter in a frying pan. After

4 minutes add the chopped duck liver and the sage leaves. Cook for 4 minutes then season with salt and freshly ground black pepper.

6 Turn the bucatini into a heated serving dish. Sprinkle with Parmesan and the strained liver and sage sauce.

7 Stir well and serve in heated dishes.

For a variation on this dish, use bigoli (p. 184) instead of bucatini. Bigoli are thicker than spaghetti; they are made with fresh pasta dough, using equal proportions of flour and fine semolina, and then pushed through a hand grinder or pasta machine.

Suggested wines

Bardolino Chiaretto, Rosato del Salento (Italy); Rosé de Loire (France); Californian Chenin Blanc (U.S.A.); Rhine Riesling (Germany).

Tortellini with creamy tomato sauce

Preparation: 2½ hours

450 g/1 lb tortellini, salt
350 g/12 oz ripe tomatoes
1 sprig rosemary
6 fresh basil leaves
250 ml/9 fl oz single cream
40 g/1½ oz butter
For the pasta
250 g/9 oz flour
3 eggs, salt

For the filling
25 g/1 oz butter
125 g/4 oz pork sausage
50 g/2 oz turkey breast
50 g/2 oz prosciutto
50 g/2 oz mortadella
1 egg
black pepper
nutmeg
125 g/4 oz grated Parmesan

1 Prepare the filling (p. 16, steps 1–6). Make the tortellini (p. 183). Cook in plenty of boiling salted water for 4 minutes or until *al dente*. Drain. Meanwhile, skin and seed the tomatoes; chop coarsely and squeeze to remove excess liquid.

2 Place the tomatoes in a frying pan with the rosemary; sprinkle with salt and cook for 8 minutes. Sieve the tomatoes or liquidize in a blender.

3 Return to the pan, add more salt if necessary, then add the basil leaves. Cook for 3 minutes.

4 Pour the cream into a large frying pan and heat gently; stir in the butter, add a little salt and heat gently for a few minutes until reduced.

5 Remove the basil leaves from the sieved tomatoes and pour into the cream and butter. Stir well.

6 Add the tortellini to the creamy tomato sauce. Stir over moderate heat for 3 minutes before serving.

Suggested wines

Pinot Spumante dell'Oltrepò Pavese, Vernaccia di San Gimignano (Italy); Champagne Blanc de Blancs (France); Californian Blanc de Noirs (U.S.A.); Chardonnay (New Zealand).

Tortellini in melted butter

Preparation: 1 hour 20 minutes

450 g/1 lb tortellini, salt
2 tbsp grated Parmesan
125 g/4 oz butter
2 fresh sage leaves

For the pasta
250 g/9 oz flour
3 eggs, salt

For the filling
25 g/1 oz butter
125 g/4 oz pork sausage
50 g/2 oz turkey breast
50 g/2 oz prosciutto
50 g/2 oz mortadella
1 egg
black pepper
nutmeg
125 g/4 oz grated Parmesan

1 Prepare the filling (p. 16, steps 1–6). Make the tortellini (p. 183). Cook in plenty of boiling salted water for 4 minutes or until *al dente*.

2 Drain well and spoon into individual heated dishes.

3 Sprinkle with the grated Parmesan.

4 Melt the butter in a small saucepan and add the sage leaves. Heat gently until the butter turns light brown.

5 Pour a little foaming butter over each dish and serve at once.

Suggested wines

Pinot Spumante di Franciacorta, Torgiano Bianco (Italy); Graves Blanc (France); Californian Chenin Blanc (U.S.A.); Müller Thurgau (Germany).

Pasta with vegetables

Tagliatelle with egg and white truffle

Preparation: 1 hour (+6 hours for the pasta to dry)

350 g/12 oz tagliatelle
80 g/3 oz butter
4 eggs
salt
50 g/2 oz grated Parmesan
50 g/2 oz white truffle

For the pasta
300 g/10 oz flour
2 eggs
1 egg yolk
salt

1 Prepare a fairly thick sheet of pasta (p. 180), combining the flour, eggs and a pinch of salt. Roll it into a sausage and cut into 8-mm/⅓-in strips. Spread the tagliatelle out carefully so that they do not stick together and leave to dry for at least 6 hours.

2 Cook the tagliatelle in plenty of boiling salted water for about 3 minutes or until *al dente*.

3 Melt the butter in a frying pan and fry the eggs, keeping the yolks soft. Sprinkle with salt. Carefully cut away the white of each egg.

4 Serve the tagliatelle in individual dishes; sprinkle with Parmesan, place an egg yolk on top and cover with a little butter. Garnish with a few pieces of thinly sliced truffle.

Suggested wines

Tocai del Collio, Torgiano Bianco (Italy); Bordeaux Blanc (France); Californian Chardonnay (U.S.A.); Rhine Sylvaner (Germany).

Tagliolini with peas and ham

Preparation: 40 minutes

275 g/10 oz egg tagliolini
700 g/1½ lb peas in the pod
salt
50 g/2 oz butter
125 g/4 oz cooked ham, thickly
  sliced

3 fresh basil leaves
1 sprig fresh parsley
3 fresh mint leaves
1 tbsp grated Parmesan
black pepper

1 Shell the peas and cook in boiling salted water for about 8 minutes. Drain.

2 Melt the butter in a saucepan. Add the peas and cook for 5 minutes. Add salt.

3 Cut the ham into 4-cm/1½-in strips.

4 Add the ham to the peas and cook for a further 8 minutes.

5 Cook the tagliolini in boiling salted water for 6 minutes or until *al dente*.

6 Finely chop the basil, parsley and mint, then sprinkle this over the peas and ham. Add the drained tagliolini.

7 Sprinkle with Parmesan and pepper and mix gently for 1 minute before serving.

Suggested wines

Pinot Bianco del Collio, Regaleali Bianco (Italy); Chablis (France); Californian Fumé Blanc (U.S.A.); Riesling (Australia).

Crêpes with radicchio Treviso style

Preparation: 1 hour

2 eggs
100 g/3½ oz flour
80 g/3 oz butter
salt
200 ml/7 fl oz milk
2–3 tbsp oil for frying
450 g/1 lb radicchio
2 shallots

150 ml/5 fl oz white wine
black pepper
25 g/1 oz grated Parmesan

For the white sauce
50 g/2 oz butter
50 g/2 oz flour
1 litre/1¾ pints milk

Suggested wines

Sylvaner dell'Alto Adige, Sauvignon del Collio (Italy);
Sancerre (France); Californian Chenin Blanc (U.S.A.);
Rhine Riesling (Germany).

1 Mix together the eggs and the flour in a bowl. Add 25 g/1 oz melted butter and a pinch of salt and gradually stir in the milk (p. 185).

2 Heat a little oil in a 20-cm/8-in non-stick frying pan. Pour in a little of the crêpe mixture and cook quickly on both sides. Remove and set aside.

3 Slice the radicchio and chop the shallots.

4 Melt 50 g/2 oz butter in a frying pan and fry the radicchio and shallots for about 15 minutes. Add the white wine, season with salt and freshly ground pepper and cook for another 10 minutes.

5 Prepare the white sauce. Melt the butter in a small saucepan, add the flour and stir for 3 minutes. Gradually pour in the hot milk and cook for 10 minutes, stirring constantly. Season with salt and white pepper.

6 Pour half the sauce into the radicchio mixture and spoon a little of this mixture into the centre of each crêpe.

7 Fold each one in four and place in a buttered ovenproof dish.

8 Cover with the remaining white sauce. Sprinkle with Parmesan and bake in a preheated oven at 220°C/425°F/mark 7 for 15 minutes.

Tortelli with truffles

Preparation: 1 hour 20 minutes

4 tortelli
50 g/2 oz grated Parmesan
50 g/2 oz butter
40 g/1½ oz white truffle
salt
For the pasta
200 g/7 oz flour
3 eggs, salt

For the filling
175 g/6 oz cooked spinach
50 g/2 oz ricotta
50 g/2 oz grated Parmesan
5 eggs
nutmeg
salt
black pepper

Suggested wines

Pinot Champenois dell'Oltrepò Pavese, Greco di Tufo
(Italy); Champagne (France); Californian Chardonnay
(U.S.A.); Moselle Riesling (Germany).

1 Make a very thin sheet of pasta (p. 180), combining the flour, eggs and a pinch of salt. Cut out eight circles, each with a diameter of 15 cm/6 in.

2 Finely chop the cooked spinach and mix with the ricotta, 50 g/2 oz grated Parmesan, 1 egg, a pinch of nutmeg, salt and freshly ground pepper. Mix well until the mixture is smooth.

3 Place four circles of dough on a sheet of waxed paper. Place a quarter of the filling in the centre of each circle.

4 Make a hollow in the spinach and place an egg yolk and about half the white in the middle.

5 Brush the edges with cold water, cover with the remaining four circles of dough and press well to seal, eliminating as much air as possible.

6 Cook the tortelli in boiling salted water for 2 minutes. Drain.

7 Place each one in a warmed serving dish and sprinkle with Parmesan.

8 Melt the butter over high heat until golden brown, then pour it over the tortelli. Garnish with the finely sliced white truffle.

Tortelli with ricotta and aubergines

Preparation: 1¼ hours

700 g/1½ lb tortelli
400 g/14 oz aubergines, salt
2–3 tbsp olive oil
50 g/2 oz butter
3 tbsp grated Parmesan
finely chopped fresh chives and
   parsley

For the pasta
250 g/9 oz flour
3 eggs, salt
For the filling
125 g/4 oz fresh ricotta
25 g/1 oz grated dried ricotta or
   Pecorino cheese
50 g/2 oz mascarpone (cream
   cheese)
salt, black pepper

1 Peel the aubergines and cut twelve slices each 8 mm/⅓ in thick. Cut the rest into 1-cm/½-in cubes. Sprinkle with salt and leave to drain in a colander for 30 minutes.

2 Make a sheet of pasta (p. 180) and cut into 6-cm/2½-in squares.

3 Mix together in a bowl the fresh and dried ricotta and the mascarpone cheese. Season with salt and pepper. Mix well and place a little of this filling on each square. Fold the corners of the square into the centre to make little packages.

4 Rinse the aubergines and pat dry. Pour a little olive oil into a frying pan and fry the aubergine slices on both sides. Sprinkle with salt, set aside and keep warm. Fry the cubed aubergines in the same way.

5 Cook the tortelli in boiling salted water for 2 minutes. Drain well. Melt the butter in a frying pan, add the tortelli and sprinkle with grated Parmesan.

6 Place 3 slices of aubergine on each warmed plate, cover with some of the tortelli and cubed aubergine. Sprinkle with chopped chives and parsley.

Suggested wines

Ribolla dei Colli Orientali del Friuli, Pinot dell'Oltrepò Pavese (Italy); Pinot d'Alsace (France); Californian Sauvignon Blanc (U.S.A.); Müller Thurgau (New Zealand).

Cannelloni niçois

Preparation: 1¼ hours

800 g/1¾ lb cannelloni, salt
1 tbsp olive oil
80 g/3 oz butter
2 tbsp grated Parmesan
3 tbsp meat juices

For the pasta
250 g/9 oz flour

2 eggs
5 tbsp white wine
salt

For the filling
450 g/1 lb spinach
3 tbsp grated Parmesan
salt
nutmeg
1 egg

1 Make a thin sheet of pasta (p. 180), combining the flour, eggs, white wine and a pinch of salt.

2 Cut the pasta into 10-cm/4-in squares.

3 Cook the pasta in plenty of boiling salted water for 2–3 minutes, adding 1 tbsp olive oil to prevent the sheets from sticking together.

4 Drain and place the squares of pasta on a clean cloth.

5 Trim and rinse the spinach and cook in a heavy saucepan with no extra water for 5–7 minutes or until tender.

6 Drain well and chop finely by hand or in a food processor.

7 Mix together in a bowl the chopped spinach, 3 tbsp grated Parmesan, a pinch of salt and nutmeg and one egg. Mix well, place a little along one side of each square and roll up.

8 Place the cannelloni in a buttered ovenproof dish. Top with 2 tbsp grated Parmesan and the rest of the butter and leave to brown in a preheated oven, 180°C/350°F/mark 4, for about 15 minutes. Brush with the meat juices and serve.

Suggested wines

Pinot Bianco del Collio, Montecarlo Bianco (Italy); Pouilly Fuissé (France); Californian Pinot Blanc (U.S.A.); Chenin Blanc (Australia).

Spinach gnocchetti with leeks and beans

Preparation: 2 hours 40 minutes (+ 12 hours for soaking the beans)

125 g/4 oz cannellini beans
salt
275 g/10 oz potatoes
225 g/8 oz spinach
2 egg yolks
125 g/4 oz flour

nutmeg
8 young leeks
125 g/4 oz butter
4 fresh basil leaves
4 fresh sage leaves
225 ml/4 fl oz white wine
6 tbsp meat juices (preferably veal)
black pepper

1 Soak the beans in cold water for 12 hours; drain, then cook in boiling water for 1¼ hours. Skin and boil the potatoes, then mash them.

2 Cook the rinsed spinach for 5–7 minutes until tender. Drain well and chop finely in a food processor.

3 Mix the chopped spinach with the potatoes; add the egg yolks, flour, a pinch of nutmeg and salt and work together until well blended.

4 Break off pieces of the mixture and roll into sausages the thickness of your finger; cut into gnocchetti.

5 Cut the leeks into 4-cm/1½-in pieces and fry gently in a frying pan in 50 g/2 oz butter. Add the basil, sage and white wine and simmer gently. Add the beans with a little of their cooking liquor and the meat juices. Simmer for a few minutes.

6 Cook the gnocchetti in boiling salted water for 2–3 minutes. Drain, season with pepper and sauté briefly in the remaining butter. Serve in very hot dishes with the beans and leeks and a little of the cooking liquid from the vegetables.

Suggested wines

Sylvaner dell'Alto Adige, Sauvignon del Collio (Italy); Sancerre (France); Californian Chenin Blanc (U.S.A.); Rhine Riesling (Germany).

Orecchiette with tomatoes and ricotta marzotica

Preparation: 1 hour (+1 day for the pasta to stand)

350 g/12 oz orecchiette
4 tbsp olive oil
1 tbsp chopped onion
1 clove garlic
400 g/14 oz tomatoes
1 sprig rosemary

salt
2 tbsp grated ricotta marzotica or Parmesan
black pepper

For the pasta
150 g/5 oz flour
150 g/5 oz fine semolina
salt, 200 ml/7 fl oz water

1 Heat the olive oil in a frying pan and add the chopped onion. Brown for 3 minutes then add the finely diced clove of garlic. Brown very gently over low heat.

2 Skin, seed and chop the tomatoes.

3 Add to the onions and garlic; add the rosemary, season with salt and cook for about 20 minutes.

4 Meanwhile, make the orecchiette (p. 184). Boil them in salted water for 5 minutes or until *al dente*. Drain well and pour into a heated tureen.

5 Pour the tomato mixture over and sprinkle with the grated ricotta. Sprinkle with freshly ground black pepper; mix well and serve.

Suggested wines

Martinafranca Bianco, Pinot Grigio dell'Alto Adige (Italy); Touraine Sauvignon (France); Californian Chardonnay (U.S.A.); Müller Thurgau (Germany).

Tortellini filled with Swiss chard

Preparation: 1 hour 20 minutes

700 g/1½ lb tortellini
salt
50 g/2 oz butter
4 tbsp grated Parmesan
black pepper

For the pasta
250 g/9 oz flour

3 eggs
salt

For the filling
400 g/14 oz Swiss chard or
    spring greens
150 g/5 oz ricotta
50 g/2 oz grated Parmesan
40 g/1½ oz butter, melted
salt, nutmeg

1 Cook the Swiss chard or greens in boiling salted water for 7–10 minutes or until tender. Drain well, allow to cool slightly, then chop finely. Mix together with the remaining filling ingredients.

2 Roll out the prepared pasta dough (p. 180), cut into 5-cm/2-in squares and place a little filling in the middle of each.

3 Fold over into a triangle; join the two side points and press them together, then fold down the third point.

4 Cook the tortellini in boiling salted water for about 4 minutes. Drain well and transfer to heated dishes.

5 Melt the butter in a small saucepan and pour it over the tortellini. Sprinkle with grated Parmesan and freshly ground pepper.

Suggested wines

Riesling dell'Oltrepò Pavese, Greco di Tufo (Italy); Graves Blanc (France); Californian Chenin Blanc (U.S.A.); Chardonnay (New Zealand).

55

Pansooti with walnut sauce

Preparation: 1½ hours

700 g/1½ lb pansooti
400 g/14 oz walnuts
50 g/2 oz fresh breadcrumbs
1 clove garlic
salt
3 tbsp olive oil
4 tbsp milk
4 tbsp grated Parmesan

For the pasta
300 g/10 oz flour
200 ml/7 fl oz white wine
salt
For the filling
600 g/1¼ lb spinach or spring
  greens
200 g/7 oz ricotta, salt
40 g/1½ oz grated Parmesan
1 egg, 1 clove garlic

Suggested wines

Riesling dei Colli Orientali del Friuli, Terlano dell'Alto
Adige (Italy); Sancerre (France); Californian Chardonnay
(U.S.A.); Rhine Riesling (Germany).

1 Cook the spinach or spring greens in the minimum of salted water. Drain and chop finely by hand or in a food processor.

2 Mix together in a bowl the chopped spinach, ricotta, 40 g/ 1½ oz Parmesan, the egg, the finely chopped garlic and a pinch of salt.

3 Prepare the pasta dough (p. 180), combining the flour, wine, 200 ml/7 fl oz warm water and a pinch of salt. Roll out into two strips. Shape the filling into little balls and place on the first sheet of pasta at 5-cm/2-in intervals.

4 Cover with the second sheet and press around the filling to seal. Cut into squares with a pastry wheel.

5 Shell the walnuts and blanch them in boiling water so that the skins can be rubbed off easily.

6 Pound the walnuts in a mortar with the soaked and squeezed breadcrumbs, the clove of garlic and a pinch of salt until you have a smooth paste.

7 Press the mixture through a fine sieve with the back of a wooden spoon. Add 3 tbsp olive oil and 4 tbsp milk.

8 Cook the pansooti in boiling salted water for about 5 minutes. Drain well and transfer to a heated serving dish. Add the 4 tbsp grated Parmesan and the walnut sauce and mix gently before serving.

Fazzoletti with basil

Preparation: 1 hour 10 minutes

400 g/14 oz fazzoletti
6 spinach leaves
50 g/2 oz fresh basil
5 tbsp olive oil
25 g/1 oz pine nuts
salt
50 g/2 oz butter

4 tbsp grated Parmesan
black pepper

For the pasta
300 g/10 oz flour
3 eggs
1 egg yolk
salt

1 Prepare a sheet of pasta (p. 180). Roll out and cut into twenty-four squares measuring 7.5 × 7.5 cm/3 × 3 in.

2 Rinse the spinach and basil, setting aside eight whole basil leaves. Place in a liquidiser with 4 tbsp olive oil, the pine nuts and a pinch of salt. Blend to a smooth paste.

3 Cook the pasta squares in boiling salted water for 3–5 minutes until *al dente*, adding 1 tbsp olive oil to prevent them from sticking.

4 Melt the butter in a frying pan. Drain the fazzoletti and add to the frying pan. Place three squares of pasta on each heated plate.

5 Spread a little of the basil sauce on top, sprinkle with Parmesan and cover with another three pieces of pasta. Sprinkle with pepper.

6 Place in the oven preheated to 150°C/300°F/mark 2 for 2 minutes. Spread ½ tbsp basil sauce on each serving and garnish with two basil leaves.

Suggested wines

Sylvaner dell'Alto Adige, Riesling dell'Oltrepò Pavese (Italy); Sancerre (France); Californian Sauvignon Blanc (U.S.A.); Riesling (Australia).

Pizzoccheri (noodles and vegetables)

Preparation: 1 hour 10 minutes

250 g/9 oz pizzoccheri
225 g/8 oz potatoes
225 g/8 oz Savoy cabbage
125 g/4 oz spring greens
salt
80 g/3 oz butter
125 g/4 oz Bitto cheese
2 tbsp grated Parmesan

black pepper
1 clove garlic

For the pasta
150 g/5 oz buckwheat flour
50 g/2 oz flour
salt
250 ml/9 fl oz milk

1 Peel and dice the potatoes. Rinse the cabbage and spring greens and cut into strips.

2 Make the pizzoccheri (p. 185). Cook the potatoes in boiling salted water for 4 minutes, then add the cabbage and spring greens. Cook for 3 minutes before adding the pizzoccheri.

3 When the noodles are *al dente*, drain and transfer to a buttered ovenproof dish. Add the thinly sliced Bitto cheese and sprinkle with Parmesan

and with freshly ground black pepper.

4 Melt the butter in a small saucepan and add the finely diced garlic. Brown gently over low heat, then pour over the noodles and vegetables. Place in a preheated oven, 170°C/325°F/mark 3, for a few minutes before serving.

Suggested wines

Lagrein Rosato dell'Alto Adige, Grignolino del Monferrato Casalese (Italy); Beaujolais (France); Californian Blanc de Noirs (U.S.A.); Rhine Sylvaner (Germany).

Pasta shells and spaghettini with tomato sauce

Preparation: 30 minutes

175 g/6 oz pasta shells
125 g/4 oz spaghettini
450 g/1 lb ripe tomatoes
6 tbsp olive oil
salt
6 leaves fresh basil
1 clove garlic
black pepper

Suggested wines

Ribolla dei Colli Orientali del Friuli, Bianchello del Metauro
(Italy); Muscadet (France); Californian Pinot Blanc (U.S.A.);
Vinho Verde Bianco (Portugal).

1 Immerse the tomatoes briefly in boiling water to loosen the skins. Skin, and discard the seeds.

2 Chop into small pieces and reserve 4 tbsp chopped tomatoes.

3 Pour 1 tbsp olive oil into a frying pan. Add most of the tomatoes, season with salt and cook for 6 minutes.

4 Press the tomatoes through a fine sieve and place in a large frying pan.

5 Add 2 tbsp oil and the basil and cook for 1 minute.

6 Cook the pasta shells in boiling salted water for 10–12 minutes. Add the spaghettini and cook for 8–10 minutes or until *al dente*.

7 Drain the pasta. Pour into the frying pan with the tomato sauce. Stir well over high heat for 1 minute then transfer to individual dishes. Place 1 tbsp raw tomatoes on each dish.

8 Finely dice the garlic and brown in the remaining oil. Spoon a little over each dish; sprinkle with freshly ground black pepper and serve.

61

Tagliolini with marrow flowers

Preparation: 1 hour

275 g/10 oz tagliolini
16 marrow flowers
2 tbsp olive oil
50 g/2 oz butter
salt
2 fresh sage leaves
1 tbsp grated Parmesan
black pepper

For the pasta
250 g/9 oz flour
3 eggs
salt

1 Rinse and dry the marrow flowers.

2 Trim off the stems, carefully open the flowers and remove the stamens.

3 Pour the olive oil and 1 tbsp butter into a frying pan. Add the marrow flowers, sprinkle with salt and cook for about 5 minutes.

4 Prepare the tagliolini (p. 181) and cook in boiling salted water for 6 minutes until *al dente*.

5 Melt the rest of the butter in a large frying pan and add the sage. Press the leaves with a fork to extract the flavour.

6 When the butter turns light brown, remove the sage. Add the tagliolini and grated Parmesan. Sprinkle with freshly ground black pepper, add the marrow flowers and stir gently before serving.

Suggested wines

Pinot Bianco del Collio, Soave (Italy); Pouilly Fumé (France); Californian Pinot Blanc (U.S.A.); Müller Thurgau (Germany).

Pappardelle and tagliolini with nettles

Preparation: 1 hour

350 g/12 oz pappardelle
50 g/2 oz tagliolini
600 g/1¼ lb nettles (leaves
 only)
salt, 50 g/2 oz butter
4 tbsp grated Parmesan
black pepper

For the pasta
350 g/12 oz flour
3 eggs
1 egg yolk
salt

1 Cook the nettles briefly in boiling salted water. Drain well.

2 Chop finely then transfer to a frying pan with 3 tbsp melted butter.

3 Prepare the pappardelle (p. 181); cook for 4 minutes in boiling salted water until *al dente*.

4 Prepare the tagliolini (p. 181); cook for 6 minutes in boiling salted water in a separate saucepan. Drain when *al dente*.

5 Add the pappardelle to the frying pan containing the nettles. Add 3 tbsp grated Parmesan and stir over high heat for 2 minutes.

6 Serve the pappardelle in heated dishes. Melt the remaining butter and add the tagliolini. Sprinkle generously with freshly ground pepper and arrange a spoonful of tagliolini in the centre of each dish.

Suggested wines

Pinot Grigio dell'Alto Adige, Greco di Tufo (Italy);
Chassagne Montrachet (France); Californian Chardonnay
(U.S.A.); Vinho Verde Bianco (Portugal).

63

Fazzoletti with marrow flowers and asparagus

Preparation: 1 hour 10 minutes

225 g/8 oz fazzoletti
350 g/12 oz asparagus
salt, 1 tbsp olive oil
4 tbsp grated Parmesan
pepper
12 marrow flowers
1 small courgette
80 g/3 oz butter

For the pasta
200 g/7 oz flour
2 eggs
salt

For the sauce
50 g/2 oz butter
40 g/1½ oz flour
250 ml/9 fl oz milk
nutmeg

Suggested wines

Sauvignon del Collio, Sylvaner dell'Alto Adige (Italy);
Sancerre (France); Californian Gewürztraminer (U.S.A.);
Riesling (Australia).

64

1 Trim and rinse the asparagus. Cut off the green tips and cook the stems in boiling salted water for about 15 minutes.

2 Drain the stems and reduce to a pulp in a liquidizer.

3 Cook the asparagus tips in boiling salted water for about 10 minutes.

4 Prepare a sheet of pasta (p. 180) and cut into eight 10-cm/4-in squares. Cook the fazzoletti in plenty of boiling salted water for 3–5 minutes, adding 1 tbsp oil to prevent them from sticking together.

5 Melt 50 g/2 oz butter in a small pan, add the flour and stir for 1 minute. Add the hot milk, and a pinch of nutmeg and cook for about 15 minutes.

6 Add the asparagus purée and season lightly with salt.

7 Place a fazzoletto in each of four dishes; arrange the asparagus tips on top, pointing outwards. Sprinkle with grated Parmesan and pepper. Place three marrow flowers on top and cover with a little sauce. Cover with a second square of pasta.

8 Garnish each dish with a few slices of courgette, sautéed in 2 tbsp butter, and two asparagus tips. Transfer to a preheated oven, 170°C/325°F/mark 3, for a few minutes. Pour 1 tbsp melted butter over each dish before serving.

Tagliolini with white truffle

Preparation: 50 minutes

400 g/14 oz tagliolini
salt
4 tbsp grated Parmesan
80 g/3 oz butter
50 g/2 oz white truffle

For the pasta
350 g/12 oz flour
3 eggs
1 egg yolk
salt

1 Prepare the tagliolini
(p. 181). Cook for 3–4 minutes
in boiling salted water.

2 Drain the tagliolini. Transfer
to heated dishes and sprinkle
with Parmesan.

3 Melt the butter in a small
saucepan and pour over the
tagliolini.

4 Sprinkle with very fine slivers
of white truffle, grated with a
mandoline cutter.

Suggested wines

Pinot Spumante del Oltrepò Pavese, Terlano dell'Alto Adige
(Italy); Bâtard Montrachet (France); Californian
Chardonnay (U.S.A.); Müller Thurgau (Germany).

Garganelli with courgettes

Preparation: 1 hour 10 minutes

400 g/14 oz garganelli
4 small courgettes, salt
50 g/2 oz butter
4 shallots
125 ml/4 fl oz white wine
2 tbsp meat juices
4 tbsp grated Parmesan
black pepper

For the pasta
250 g/9 oz flour
150 g/5 oz fine semolina
4 eggs
salt

1 Cut the courgettes into thin slices 5 × 3 mm/2 × ⅛ in.

2 Prepare the garganelli (p. 186) and cook for 5 minutes in boiling salted water until *al dente*. Drain.

3 Meanwhile, sauté the courgette slices briefly in half the butter until tender but still crisp. Sprinkle with salt.

4 Finely slice the shallots and brown gently in the remaining butter in a frying pan. Pour in the wine, add the meat juices and sprinkle with salt. Cook for 5 minutes.

5 Add the garganelli to the frying pan; sprinkle with Parmesan and pepper and cook over high heat for 2 minutes, shaking the pan.

6 Serve in heated dishes and garnish with the sautéed courgettes.

Suggested wines

Verdicchio dei Castelli di Jesi, Riesling dei Colli Orientali del Friuli (Italy); Pouilly Fuissé (France); Californian Sauvignon Blanc (U.S.A.); Moselle Riesling (Germany).

Penne with peppers and courgettes

Preparation: 30 minutes

275 g/10 oz fluted penne
1 sweet yellow pepper
2 small courgettes
40 g/1½ oz butter
salt
225 g/8 oz freshly made tomato
    sauce
4 courgette flowers

25 g/1 oz flour
150 ml/5 fl oz vegetable oil
1 tbsp chopped fresh parsley
black pepper

1 Scorch the pepper over high heat until the skin blisters, then rub off.

2 Skin the courgettes and cut them and the pepper into small dice.

3 Melt the butter in a large frying pan; add the diced pepper and fry for 5 minutes. Add the courgettes, sprinkle with salt and fry until the vegetables are tender but still crisp. Stir in the tomato sauce.

4 Dip the courgette flowers in flour and fry briefly in vegetable oil. Drain. Sprinkle with salt.

5 Cook the penne in plenty of boiling salted water for 10–12 minutes until *al dente*.

6 Drain and add to the frying pan with the vegetables. Stir and sprinkle with chopped parsley and freshly ground black pepper. Garnish each serving with a fried courgette flower.

Suggested wines

Sylvaner dell'Alto Adige, Sauvignon del Collio (Italy); Gewürztraminer d'Alsace (France); Californian Johannisberg Riesling (U.S.A.); Chenin Blanc (Australia).

69

Maccheroncini with peas

Preparation: 40 minutes

275 g/10 oz maccheroncini
400 g/14 oz fresh peas
50 g/2 oz butter
salt
2 tbsp grated Parmesan

1 tbsp chopped fresh parsley
black pepper

1 Shell the peas.

2 Melt half the butter in a large frying pan. Add the peas, sprinkle with salt and cook for about 20 minutes until tender.

3 Cook the maccheroncini in boiling salted water for 10–12 minutes or until *al dente*. Drain and add to the pan with the peas.

4 Add the Parmesan, chopped parsley, the remaining butter and a sprinkling of pepper. Mix well before serving.

Suggested wines

Gavi, Trebbiano di Romagna (Italy); Muscadet (France); Californian Chenin Blanc (U.S.A.); Moselle Riesling (Germany).

Rigatoni with basil

Preparation: 20 minutes

350 g/12 oz rigatoni
salt
8 tbsp olive oil
50 g/2 oz fresh basil
1 clove garlic

2 tbsp grated Parmesan
1 tbsp grated Pecorino cheese
black pepper

1 Cook the rigatoni for 10–12 minutes in boiling salted water until *al dente*. Drain well.

2 Heat the olive oil gently in a large frying pan.

3 Finely chop the basil and garlic and heat gently in the oil for 2 minutes.

4 Add the rigatoni to the frying pan and sprinkle with grated Parmesan and Pecorino.

5 Stir well, sprinkle with pepper and serve at once.

Suggested wines

Gavi, Riesling dell'Oltrepò Pavese (Italy); Sancerre (France); Californian Sauvignon Blanc (U.S.A.); Rhine Riesling (Germany).

Ravioli filled with mushrooms

Preparation: 1½ hours

600 g/1¼ lb ravioli, salt
50 g/2 oz butter
4 fresh sage leaves
2–3 sprigs fresh thyme or ½ tsp
  dried
40 g/1½ oz grated Parmesan
For the pasta
250 g/9 oz flour

3 eggs, salt

For the filling
225 g/8 oz mushrooms
40 g/1½ oz butter
1 clove garlic, salt
125 g/4 oz ricotta
1 tsp chopped fresh parsley
2 tbsp grated Parmesan
black pepper, 1 egg white

Suggested wines

Pinot Bianco del Collio, Vernaccia di San Gimignano
(Italy); Montrachet (France); Californian Johannisberg
Riesling (U.S.A.); Rhine Sylvaner (Germany).

1 Rinse, dry and cut the mushrooms into strips.

2 Melt 40 g/1½ oz butter in a frying pan. Add the mushrooms, crushed garlic and a pinch of salt and cook until the mushrooms are tender.

3 Mix together in a bowl the ricotta, mushrooms, chopped parsley and Parmesan. Sprinkle with freshly ground black pepper and stir well.

4 Prepare the pasta (p. 180) and cut into 5-cm/2-in squares using a pastry wheel.

5 Roll the filling into little balls and place one in the centre of each square of pasta. Brush the edges with water or egg white and fold over to form a triangle. Press the edges firmly together.

6 Put into boiling salted water and cook for 5 minutes or until *al dente*. Drain and serve in heated dishes.

7 Meanwhile, melt 50 g/2 oz butter in a small frying pan and soften the sage leaves and thyme.

8 Sprinkle the ravioli with grated Parmesan and cover with the strained butter.

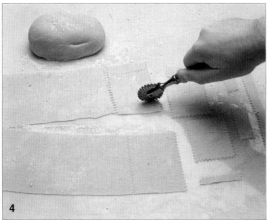

Bucatini and broccoli

Preparation: 30 minutes

275 g/10 oz bucatini
800 g/1¾ lb broccoli
salt
8 tbsp olive oil
¼ red chilli pepper
1 clove garlic
50 g/2 oz salted anchovies

1 Rinse and trim the broccoli, keeping only the tops.

2 Cook them in boiling salted water for 8–10 minutes until tender but still crisp. Drain, reserving the water, and keep warm.

3 Cook the bucatini in the reserved water for 10–12 minutes.

4 When almost *al dente* return the broccoli to the water. Drain after 2 minutes.

5 Pour the olive oil into a large frying pan. Add the chopped chilli pepper, the finely diced garlic and the rinsed, boned and chopped anchovies.

6 Heat for 3 minutes then add the bucatini and broccoli. Stir gently for 1 minute then serve. Sprinkle with grated Parmesan if desired.

Suggested wines

Riesling dei Colli Orientali del Friuli, Martinafranca Bianco (Italy); Montrachet (France); Californian Sauvignon Blanc (U.S.A.); Müller Thurgau (Germany).

Spaghettini with tomato sauce

Preparation: 30 minutes

350 g/12 oz spaghettini
½ onion
1 clove garlic
8 tbsp olive oil
400 g/14 oz ripe tomatoes
salt
black pepper

1 tbsp chopped fresh basil
20 fresh basil leaves

1 Finely chop the onion and garlic and fry briefly in the olive oil in a frying pan.

2 Skin and seed the tomatoes and cut into strips. Sprinkle with salt and add to the onions. Cover and cook gently for 5–8 minutes.

3 Cook the spaghettini in a large saucepan of boiling salted water for 8–10 minutes until *al dente*. Drain.

4 Pour the spaghettini into the sauce; sprinkle with freshly ground black pepper, stir well and add the chopped basil.

5 Serve in heated dishes and garnish with the whole basil leaves.

Suggested wines

Pinot Bianco del Collio, Bianchello del Metauro (Italy); Bordeaux Blanc (France); Californian Sauvignon Blanc (U.S.A.); Müller Thurgau (Germany).

Orecchiette with turnip tops

Preparation: 1 hour (+24 hours for the pasta to stand)

400 g/14 oz orecchiette
400 g/14 oz turnip tops
salt
125 ml/4 fl oz olive oil
black pepper

For the pasta
200 g/7 oz flour
200 g/7 oz fine semolina
salt
1¼ cups water

1 Rinse and trim the turnip tops.

2 Pour the prepared orecchiette (p. 184) into boiling salted water.

3 After 2 minutes add the turnip tops to the same saucepan.

4 Cook for a further 3–5 minutes until the turnip tops are tender, then drain.

5 Transfer to a heated serving dish and pour over the olive oil.

6 Sprinkle with freshly ground black pepper and mix gently before serving.

Suggested wines

Martinafranca Bianco, Ischia Bianco (Italy); Bourgogne Blanc (France); Californian Pinot Blanc (U.S.A.); Fumé Blanc (South Africa).

Spaghettini with tomato, garlic and parsley

Preparation: 20 minutes

275 g/10 oz spaghettini
225 g/8 oz tomatoes
6 tbsp olive oil
salt
1 sprig rosemary
½ red chilli pepper

2 cloves garlic
2 tbsp chopped fresh parsley

1 Skin and seed the tomatoes, then chop coarsely.

2 Heat 1 tbsp olive oil in a saucepan. Add the chopped tomatoes, season with salt, add the sprig of rosemary and cook for 7 minutes.

3 Cook the spaghettini in boiling salted water for 8–10 minutes until *al dente*. Drain.

4 Heat the remaining oil in a large frying pan. Add the finely chopped chilli pepper and the finely diced garlic and brown gently over low heat.

5 Turn the spaghettini into the frying pan with the chilli and garlic-flavoured oil and add the chopped parsley.

6 Push the tomatoes through a sieve with the back of a wooden spoon, then reheat the purée. Pour this over the pasta, mix well and serve.

Suggested wines

Pinot di Franciacorta, Regaleali Bianco (Italy); Puligny Montrachet (France); Californian Gewürztraminer (U.S.A.); Rhine Riesling (Germany).

Penne with asparagus

Preparation: 30 minutes

275 g/10 oz penne
450 g/1 lb asparagus
salt
50 g/2 oz butter
1 tbsp chopped fresh parsley
3 tbsp grated Parmesan
black pepper

1 Trim, rinse and tie the asparagus in two bundles.

2 Stand them upright in a tall saucepan and simmer in lightly salted water for 5–10 minutes until tender but still crisp.

3 Drain and hold in a colander under cold running water for 2 minutes to cool.

4 Untie the bundles, cut off the woody stems and cut the asparagus into 2.5-cm/1-in pieces.

5 Melt half the butter in a large frying pan. Add the asparagus and cook over moderate heat for 2 minutes. Add a little salt if necessary.

6 Meanwhile, cook the penne in boiling salted water for 10–12 minutes or until *al dente*.

7 Drain the penne and add to the asparagus in the frying pan.

8 Stir in the remaining butter, chopped parsley, Parmesan and freshly ground black pepper. Stir over heat for another 2 minutes.

Suggested wines

Pinot Bianco del Collio, Vermentino (Italy); Puligny Montrachet (France); Californian Chardonnay (U.S.A.); Moselle Riesling (Germany).

Tortelli with pumpkin

Preparation: 1¾ hours

800 g/1¾ lb pumpkin
50 g/2 oz macaroons (amaretti)
100 g/3½ oz sweet fruit pickle
   (Cremona mustard)
6 tbsp grated Parmesan
nutmeg
salt

black pepper
½ cup butter

For the pasta
250 g/9 oz flour
3 eggs
salt

Suggested wines

Pinot Champenois di Franciacorta, Sylvaner dell'Alto Adige
(Italy); Montrachet (France); Californian Sauvignon Blanc
(U.S.A.); Rhine Riesling (Germany).

1 Cut the pumpkin into slices and discard the seeds. Remove the rind and bake the slices in the oven for 20 minutes.

2 Press the pumpkin through a fine sieve with the back of a wooden spoon.

3 Crush the macaroons and mix with the minced sweet fruit pickle, 2 tbsp grated Parmesan and a pinch of nutmeg. Season with salt and pepper and stir well.

4 Prepare a sheet of pasta dough (p. 180) and roll out into two layers. Using a knife score the bottom sheet into twenty 10-cm/4-in squares. Place a ball of filling in the centre of each square.

5 Cover with the second sheet of dough; press round the edges of each square to seal, then cut out the tortelli with a pastry wheel.

6 Cook the tortelli in boiling salted water for 2 minutes.

7 Remove them one at a time from the saucepan, using a slotted spoon. Drain and place on warmed plates.

8 Sprinkle with grated Parmesan and spoon a little melted butter over the top.

Maccheroncini with sweet peppers

Preparation: 30 minutes

275 g/10 oz maccheroncini
350 g/12 oz sweet red and
    yellow peppers
8 tbsp olive oil
salt
5 tbsp grated Parmesan
black pepper

1 Hold the whole peppers over a flame or place under the grill until the skin blisters.

2 Rub off the skins. (Immersing the peppers in warm water may make this easier.)

3 Cut the peppers in half, discard the seeds and cut into thin strips.

4 Pour half the olive oil into a large frying pan. Add the peppers, sprinkle with salt and cook over moderate heat for about 8 minutes until the peppers are tender but still crisp.

5 Meanwhile, cook the maccheroncini in boiling salted water for 10–12 minutes until *al dente*. Drain.

6 Pour the drained pasta into the frying pan. Add the grated Parmesan, freshly ground black pepper and the remaining oil and heat for 1 minute, stirring constantly. Serve.

Suggested wines

Ischia Bianco, Spumante Champenois del Trentino (Italy); Gewürztraminer d'Alsace (France); Californian Johannisberg Riesling (U.S.A.); Rhine Sylvaner (Germany).

Ditalini with mixed vegetables

Preparation: 40 minutes

275 g/10 oz ditalini
1 sweet yellow pepper
8 tbsp olive oil
1 carrot
salt
1 courgette
125 g/4 oz green beans

1 tbsp chopped fresh parsley
2 tbsp grated Parmesan
black pepper

1 Hold the pepper over a flame or place under the grill until the skin blisters and can be rubbed off.

2 Cut into strips and fry gently in half the olive oil in a large frying pan.

3 Peel and rinse the carrot; cut into thin slices and cook in boiling salted water for a few minutes until tender. Drain and add to the pepper in the frying pan.

4 Thinly slice the courgette and add to the frying pan.

5 Trim the green beans; cook in boiling salted water for a few minutes until tender, then add to the other vegetables.

6 Cook the ditalini in boiling salted water for 10–12 minutes or until *al dente*. Drain and add to the vegetables.

7 Pour the remaining oil into the frying pan. Add the chopped parsley, Parmesan and freshly ground black pepper. Stir for 2 minutes over heat before serving.

Suggested wines

Corvo di Salaparuta, Riesling dell'Oltrepò Pavese (Italy); Meursault (France); Californian Gewürztraminer (U.S.A.); Rhine Sylvaner (Germany).

Pappardelle with mushroom sauce

Preparation: 1 hour 20 minutes
  (+2 hours for soaking the
  mushrooms)
350 g/12 oz pappardelle
50 g/2 oz dried *porcini*
1 tbsp olive oil
1 clove garlic, salt
2 tbsp grated Parmesan
black pepper

For the pasta
300 g/10 oz flour
3 eggs
salt
For the sauce
50 g/2 oz butter
1 tbsp flour
250 ml/9 fl oz hot milk
salt

1 Soak the dried mushrooms for 2 hours in warm water, stirring occasionally to loosen any dirt.

2 Strain the water in which the mushrooms were soaked and reserve, taking care to discard any sediment. Coarsely chop the drained mushrooms.

3 Heat the olive oil in a large frying pan. Add the crushed garlic, chopped mushrooms and a sprinkling of salt and heat gently, gradually adding the reserved water in which the mushrooms were soaked.

4 Meanwhile, prepare a white sauce: melt the butter in a saucepan. Stir in the flour and mix well over heat. Stir for 1 minute before gradually adding the hot milk. Stir constantly. Season with salt, bring to the boil, then simmer gently for 10 minutes, stirring constantly.

5 Pour the white sauce into the mushrooms and stir well.

6 Prepare the pappardelle (see p. 181) and cook in boiling salted water for 4 minutes until *al dente*. Drain and pour into the frying pan with the mushrooms. Add the Parmesan and freshly ground black pepper and mix well over high heat for 2 minutes.

Suggested wines

Pinot Grigio dell'Alto Adige, Tocai del Collio (Italy); Montrachet (France); Californian Chardonnay (U.S.A.); Chenin Blanc (South Africa).

Pasta wheels with mixed vegetables

Preparation: 30 minutes

275 g/10 oz pasta wheels
2 large ripe tomatoes
6 tbsp olive oil
salt
1 medium carrot
175 g/6 oz green beans

1 medium courgette
½ tsp oregano
black pepper

1 Skin the tomatoes, discard the seeds and cut into dice. Heat in 1 tbsp olive oil for 8 minutes, sprinkled with salt. Push through a sieve or liquidize.

2 Peel the carrot and slice finely. Trim the beans and cook both vegetables in boiling salted water for 4 minutes.

3 Rinse the courgette and slice finely. Place in a large frying pan with 2 tbsp oil; sprinkle with salt and cook for about 4 minutes.

4 Drain the carrots and beans. Cut the beans in half and add both vegetables to the frying pan with the remaining oil. Cook for about 4 minutes.

5 Cook the pasta wheels for 10–12 minutes in plenty of boiling salted water until *al dente*.

6 Add the drained pasta to the vegetables. Pour over the tomato sauce and sprinkle with the oregano and freshly ground black pepper. Stir well over high heat for 2 minutes before serving.

Suggested wines

Verdicchio dei Castelli di Jesi, Gavi (Italy); Californian Pinot Bianco (U.S.A.); Chablis (France); Vinho Verde Bianco (Portugal).

Pennette with courgettes

Preparation: 30 minutes

275 g/10 oz pennette
4 medium courgettes
6 tbsp olive oil
salt
1 tbsp chopped fresh parsley
black pepper

1 Rinse the courgettes and slice finely.

2 Pour the olive oil into a large frying pan; add the courgettes, cover and cook for a few minutes. Sprinkle with salt and cook over moderate heat until tender but still slightly crisp.

3 Meanwhile, cook the pennette in plenty of boiling salted water for 8–10 minutes until *al dente*.

4 Drain the pasta and add to the frying pan. Sprinkle with the parsley and freshly ground black pepper and mix well before serving.

Suggested wines

Tocai del Collio, Soave (Italy); Chablis (France); Californian Pinot Blanc (U.S.A.); Moselle Riesling (Germany).

Pasta spirals with artichokes, peppers and mushrooms

Preparation: 30 minutes

275 g/10 oz pasta spirals
1 artichoke
salt
125 g/4 oz button mushrooms
½ sweet red pepper

150 ml/5 fl oz olive oil
2 tbsp grated Parmesan
black pepper

Suggested wines

Pinot dell'Oltrepò Pavese, Montecarlo Bianco (Italy);
Bordeaux Blanc (France); Californian Gewürztraminer
(U.S.A.); Sauvignon Blanc (South Africa).

1 Cut off and discard any hard outer leaves and trim the sharp tips from the remaining leaves of the artichoke.

2 Cut the artichoke in half, cut out and discard the hairy choke in the middle, then cut the head into slices.

3 Blanch the sliced artichoke in salted water for 2 minutes; add the trimmed and rinsed mushrooms and cook for a further 3 minutes.

4 Hold the pepper over a flame until the skin blisters and can be rubbed off.

5 Cut the skinned pepper into strips and then dice.

6 Heat half the olive oil in a large frying pan. Add the diced pepper, sprinkle with salt and fry gently until tender.

7 Add the drained artichoke slices and diced mushrooms to the frying pan. Sprinkle with salt and continue to cook, stirring, until the vegetables are tender.

8 Meanwhile, cook the pasta spirals in boiling salted water for 10–12 minutes until *al dente*. Drain and pour into the frying pan with the remaining oil, grated Parmesan and a sprinkling of freshly ground black pepper. Mix well before serving.

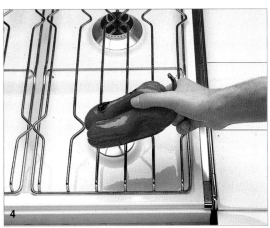

Penne with black olives and tomatoes

Preparation: 30 minutes

275 g/10 oz penne
350 g/12 oz ripe tomatoes
6 tbsp olive oil
salt
125 g/4 oz black olives
½ tsp oregano

1 tbsp grated Pecorino cheese
black pepper
4 leaves fresh basil

1 Skin the tomatoes and discard the seeds.

2 Chop coarsely and heat in the olive oil in a large frying pan. Sprinkle with salt.

3 After 6 minutes, add the pitted olives and the oregano. Cook for a further 5 minutes.

4 Cook the penne in boiling salted water for 10–12 minutes until *al dente*. Drain.

5 Add the penne to the tomatoes and olives. Sprinkle with the Pecorino and freshly ground black pepper and stir well over high heat for 2 minutes.

6 Turn into a heated serving dish and garnish with fresh basil.

Suggested wines

Orvieto, Pinot di Franciacorta (Italy); Pouilly Fuissé (France); Californian Chenin Blanc (U.S.A.); Moselle Riesling (Germany).

Pasta shells with mushrooms and artichokes

Preparation: 30 minutes

275 g/10 oz pasta shells
2 young artichokes
150 ml/5 fl oz olive oil
2 cloves garlic
225 g/8 oz mushrooms
   (preferably porcini)
salt
black pepper

1 Cut off and discard any hard outer leaves and trim the sharp points from the remaining leaves of the artichokes. Cut into thin strips, discarding any hairs; rinse and dry.

2 Heat in a frying pan for 5 minutes in 6 tbsp oil with a crushed clove of garlic.

3 Trim, rinse and dry the mushrooms and cut into pieces.

4 Add the mushrooms to the artichokes, sprinkle with salt and cook for 7–10 minutes. The vegetables should be tender but still crisp.

5 Cook the pasta shells in boiling salted water for 10–12 minutes or *al dente*. Drain and add to the frying pan.

6 Heat the remaining oil in a saucepan and add the remaining diced garlic. Brown lightly then pour the oil over the pasta. Sprinkle with pepper, mix well and serve.

Suggested wines

Pinot Champenois dell'Oltrepò Pavese, Sauvignon del Collio (Italy); Gewürztraminer d'Alsace (France); Californian Johannisberg Riesling (U.S.A.); Rhine Sylvaner (Germany).

Ravioli with aubergine and thyme filling

Preparation: 1½ hours

800 g/1¾ lb ravioli
salt
125 g/4 oz butter
½ tsp fresh thyme
For the pasta
250 g/9 oz flour
1 tbsp oil
3 eggs, salt

For the filling
½ onion
350 g/12 oz aubergines
80 g/3 oz butter
salt
2 small courgettes
50 g/2 oz ricotta
50 g/2 oz goat's cheese
1 egg

Suggested wines

Torbato, Torgiano Bianco (Italy); Meursault (France);
Californian Chardonnay (U.S.A.); Müller Thurgau
(Germany).

1 Finely chop the onion; skin and dice the aubergines.

2 Melt 40 g/1½ oz butter in a frying pan. Add the onions and aubergines, sprinkle with salt and cook until tender.

3 Cut the courgettes into large matchsticks. Heat 40 g/1½ oz butter in a frying pan and fry the courgettes until crisp.

4 Push the aubergines and half the courgettes through a sieve with the back of a wooden spoon, or blend in a liquidizer.

5 Mix this purée of vegetables with the ricotta, goat's cheese, the egg and salt and stir until smooth and well blended.

6 Roll out the prepared pasta dough (p. 180) and cut into rectangles. Place a little of the filling in the centre of each; fold over the edge and press to seal, then twist both ends, like wrapped sweets.

7 Cook the ravioli in boiling salted water for 5 minutes. Drain well and serve on individual heated plates.

8 Melt 125 g/4 oz butter and pour it over the ravioli. Sprinkle with fresh thyme and garnish with the remaining courgettes.

Tagliatelle
with mushrooms

Preparation: 1 hour

350 g/12 oz tagliatelle
350 g/12 oz mushrooms
salt
50 g/2 oz butter
1 clove garlic
2 tbsp grated Parmesan

1 tbsp chopped fresh parsley
black pepper

For the pasta
300 g/10 oz flour
3 eggs
salt

1 Rinse and trim the mushrooms.

2 Cook in boiling salted water for 4 minutes.

3 Drain and cut into small pieces.

4 Melt the butter in a frying pan; add the crushed garlic and the mushrooms. Sprinkle with salt and cook gently for about 20 minutes.

5 Cook the prepared tagliatelle (p. 181) in boiling salted water for 3 minutes or until *al dente*.

6 Drain and add to the mushrooms together with the Parmesan, chopped parsley and a sprinkling of pepper. Mix well and serve.

Suggested wines

Terlano dell'Alto Adige, Sauvignon del Collio (Italy); Montrachet (France); Californian Johannisberg Riesling (U.S.A.); Rhine Riesling (Germany).

Trenette with pesto (basil sauce)

Preparation: 1 hour 10 minutes

275 g/10 oz trenette
125 g/4 oz potatoes
50 g/2 oz green beans
salt
8 tbsp pesto sauce (p. 178)
2 tbsp grated Pecorino cheese

1 Skin, rinse and cut the potatoes into cubes. Rinse and slice the beans.

2 Cook the vegetables in boiling salted water until tender. Drain, reserving the cooking water, and keep hot.

3 Cook the trenette in the reserved water for 8–10 minutes or until *al dente*.

4 Drain and add to the vegetables. Stir in the pesto and grated cheese and mix well before serving.

Suggested wines

Sauvignon del Collio, Sylvaner dell'Alto Adige (Italy); Montrachet (France); Californian Johannisberg Riesling (U.S.A.); Rhine Sylvaner (Germany).

Maccheroncini with aubergines

Preparation: 1 hour

275 g/10 oz maccheroncini
400 g/14 oz aubergines
175 ml/6 fl oz olive oil
1 clove garlic
350 g/12 oz tomatoes
salt

1 tbsp chopped fresh basil
2 tbsp dried ricotta, grated
black pepper

1 Slice the aubergines then cut into small dice.

2 Pour half the olive oil into a large frying pan, add the crushed garlic clove and the diced aubergine and fry gently until tender.

3 Skin the tomatoes, remove the seeds and chop coarsely.

4 Pour the remaining oil into a frying pan, add the tomatoes and cook over high heat for 5 minutes until slightly reduced. Add salt and the chopped basil and cook for another minute.

5 Meanwhile, cook the maccheroncini in boiling salted water for 10–12 minutes until *al dente*, then drain. Add to the tomatoes and stir in the aubergines.

6 Sprinkle with grated ricotta and black pepper and mix well before serving.

Suggested wines

Frascati, Bianchello del Metauro (Italy); Chassagne Montrachet (France); Californian Johannisberg Riesling (U.S.A.); Rhine Riesling (Germany).

Bucatini with artichokes

Preparation: 45 minutes

275 g/10 oz bucatini
4 artichokes
1 lemon
125 ml/4 fl oz olive oil
1 clove garlic
salt

1 tbsp chopped fresh parsley
black pepper
1 tbsp grated Pecorino cheese

1 Pull off any hard outer leaves and trim the pointed tips of the remaining artichoke leaves.

2 Cut the artichokes in half lengthwise, remove and discard the hairy choke from the middle, then cut into slices. Place in a bowl of water acidulated with the juice of a lemon to prevent discoloration.

3 Heat the olive oil in a large frying pan and add the crushed garlic clove.

4 When the garlic is lightly browned, add the drained artichokes. Sprinkle with salt and cook for 20 minutes, adding a little water when necessary.

5 Meanwhile, cook the bucatini in boiling salted water for 10–12 minutes until *al dente*, then drain. Pour into the frying pan with the artichokes; sprinkle with chopped parsley, freshly ground black pepper and grated Pecorino and mix well before serving.

Suggested wines

Pinot Grigio dell'Alto Adige, Regaleali Bianco (Italy); Bourgogne Blanc (France); Californian Chardonnay (U.S.A.); Chenin Blanc (New Zealand).

Spaghettini with garlic, oil and chilli pepper

Preparation: 20 minutes

350 g/12 oz spaghettini
4 cloves garlic
175 ml/6 fl oz olive oil
½ red chilli pepper
salt
1 tbsp chopped fresh parsley

1 Skin and finely dice the cloves of garlic. Place in a large frying pan with the olive oil.

2 Cut the chilli pepper into very fine rings, discarding the seeds, and add to the frying pan with the garlic. Fry very gently for 2 minutes.

3 Cook the spaghettini in boiling salted water for 8–10 minutes until *al dente*.

4 Drain and pour into the frying pan. Add the chopped parsley and mix well for 2 minutes over heat before serving.

Suggested wines

Martinafranca Bianco, Torbato (Italy); Sancerre (France); Californian Sauvignon Blanc (U.S.A.); Moselle Riesling (Germany).

Spaghettini with truffles and asparagus

Preparation: 40 minutes

275 g/10 oz spaghettini
450 g/1 lb young green
  asparagus
salt
50 g/2 oz butter

2 tbsp grated Parmesan
black pepper
50 g/2 oz black truffle

1 Trim the hard ends of the asparagus; rinse and tie into a bundle.

2 Cook upright in a tall saucepan with boiling salted water to come no more than two-thirds up the stalks of the asparagus.

3 When tender, after 10–12 minutes, drain, cut off the tips and sauté over moderate heat in half the butter, melted in a saucepan.

4 Cook the spaghettini in boiling salted water for 8–10 minutes until *al dente*. Drain.

5 Melt the remaining butter in a large saucepan; add the spaghettini, sprinkle with grated Parmesan and freshly ground black pepper and serve on individual plates.

6 Arrange a few asparagus tips decoratively on each plate and garnish with very fine slices of black truffle grated with a mandoline cutter.

Suggested wines

Pinot di Franciacorta, Riesling Renano dei Colli Orientali del Friuli (Italy); Gewürztraminer d'Alsace (France); Californian Sauvignon Blanc (U.S.A.); Müller Thurgau (Germany).

Pasta bows with beetroot

Preparation: 30 minutes

275 g/10 oz pasta bows
40 g/1½ oz butter
½ onion
125 ml/4 fl oz white wine
350 g/12 oz cooked beetroot
1 tbsp lemon juice
6 tbsp single cream

salt
2 tbsp grated Parmesan
black pepper
10 fresh basil leaves

1 Melt half the butter in a frying pan, add the finely sliced onion and fry for 3 minutes.

2 Add the white wine and cook for a further 3 minutes, then add the skinned and diced beetroot. Cook for 5 minutes.

3 Put the beetroot, lemon juice and cream into a liquidizer and blend to a smooth purée.

4 Cook the pasta bows in boiling salted water for 10–12 minutes until *al dente*, then drain.

5 Pour the beetroot purée into a large frying pan, add the remaining butter and cook for 3 minutes. Pour the pasta bows into the frying pan.

6 Sprinkle with grated Parmesan and freshly ground black pepper and stir over high heat for 2 minutes. Pour into a heated tureen to serve and garnish with finely shredded fresh basil.

Suggested wines

Tocai del Collio, Pinot dell'Oltrepò Pavese (Italy); Bordeaux Blanc (France); Müller Thurgau (Germany); Chenin Blanc (New Zealand).

Paglia e fieno (straw and hay)

Preparation: 1 hour

200 g/7 oz yellow tagliolini
200 g/7 oz green tagliolini
salt
40 g/1½ oz butter
150 ml/5 fl oz single cream
2 tbsp grated Parmesan

For the pasta
300 g/10 oz flour
3 eggs
225 g/8 oz spinach
salt

1 Prepare the yellow and green tagliolini (p. 181).

2 Cook together in boiling salted water for 4–6 minutes or until just *al dente*, then drain.

3 Heat the butter, cream and a pinch of salt for 2 minutes in a large frying pan.

4 Pour the tagliolini into the frying pan. Add the Parmesan and stir for 2 minutes over high heat before serving.

Suggested wines

Orvieto, Pinot Bianco del Collio (Italy); Bourgogne Blanc (France); Californian Chenin Blanc (U.S.A.); Chardonnay (Australia).

Tagliatelle au gratin

Preparation: 1 hour 10 minutes

400 g/14 oz spinach tagliatelle
80 g/3 oz butter
40 g/1½ oz flour
300 ml/10 fl oz milk
salt, white pepper
6 tbsp grated Parmesan

For the pasta
300 g/10 oz flour
450 g/1 lb spinach
3 eggs
salt

1 Melt 40 g/1½ oz butter in a saucepan. Stir in the flour and gradually add the hot milk; cook for 10 minutes, stirring constantly. Season with salt and white pepper.

2 Cook the tagliatelle (p. 181) in boiling salted water for 3 minutes until *al dente*.

3 Butter an ovenproof dish and pour in one-third of the tagliatelle. Cover with one-third of the white sauce and Parmesan. Continue layering until all the ingredients are used up.

4 Place flakes of butter on top and bake in a preheated oven at 170°C/325°F/mark 3 for 8 minutes before serving.

Suggested wines

Trebbiano di Romagna, Frascati (Italy); Pinot d'Alsace (France); Californian Pinot Blanc (U.S.A.); Chardonnay (South Africa).

Tagliolini with mushrooms

Preparation: 1 hour

350 g/12 oz tagliolini
350 g/12 oz mushrooms,
　preferably porcini
salt
125 ml/4 fl oz olive oil
1 clove garlic
6 fresh basil leaves
1 tbsp chopped fresh parsley

1 tbsp grated Parmesan
black pepper

For the pasta
300 g/10 oz flour
3 eggs
salt

1 Wash the mushrooms in salted water; drain and then slice.

2 Heat 5 tbsp olive oil in a large frying pan and gently fry the mushrooms for 5–8 minutes or until tender. Sprinkle with salt.

3 Cook the tagliolini (p. 181) in plenty of boiling salted water for 3–4 minutes if freshly made, for 6 minutes if dried. Drain.

4 Brown the finely diced garlic in the remaining oil over low heat for 2 minutes.

5 Pour the tagliolini into the frying pan containing the mushrooms, keeping the heat low. Add the garlic and oil, the finely chopped basil and parsley and the grated Parmesan. Stir well, adding a little of the cooking water from the tagliolini if necessary. Sprinkle with freshly ground black pepper before serving.

Suggested wines

Pinot Bianco di Franciacorta, Pinot Grigio dell'Alto Adige (Italy); Montrachet (France); Californian Chardonnay (U.S.A.); Chenin Blanc (South Africa).

Pasta with cheese and eggs

Spaghetti with Sardinian Pecorino cheese

Preparation: 40 minutes

275 g/10 oz spaghetti
4 tbsp olive oil
1 clove garlic
275 g/10 oz ripe tomatoes
salt
2 tbsp chopped fresh parsley
1 tbsp chopped fresh basil
black pepper

25 g/1 oz butter
125 g/4 oz mild Sardinian
   Pecorino cheese

1 Heat the olive oil in a frying pan and brown the garlic gently for a few minutes.

2 Add the skinned, seeded and chopped tomatoes; sprinkle with salt and cook for 15 minutes.

3 Trim, rinse and finely chop the parsley and basil.

4 Add to the tomatoes and cook for 3 minutes.

5 Cook the spaghetti in boiling salted water for 10–12 minutes or until *al dente*. Drain, mix with the tomato sauce and spoon into individual buttered ovenproof dishes. Sprinkle generously with freshly ground black pepper, and a few flakes of butter.

6 Thinly slice the Pecorino, place on top of each portion of spaghetti and bake in a preheated oven, 170°C/325°F/ mark 3, until the cheese melts.

Suggested wines

Torbato, Montecarlo Bianco (Italy); Meursault (France); Californian Chardonnay (U.S.A.); Sauvignon Blanc (South Africa).

Creamy potato gnocchi

Preparation: 1¼ hours

600 g/1¼ lb potatoes
salt
100 g/3½ oz flour
50 g/2 oz grated Parmesan
125 g/4 oz Fontina Valdostana
   cheese
200 ml/7 fl oz single cream

1 Cook the potatoes in their skins in salted water for 15–20 minutes or until tender. Skin, then mash and allow to cool slightly before stirring in the flour.

2 Shape the mixture into small sausages about 2.5 cm/1 in in diameter.

3 Cut the sausages into 3-cm/1¼-in lengths and roll them over the prongs of a fork, pressing with the thumb to give a ridged effect.

4 Cook the gnocchi in boiling water and remove with a slotted spoon when they rise to the surface.

5 Transfer to a buttered ovenproof dish, sprinkle with grated Parmesan and place the thinly sliced Valdostana cheese on top. Cover with the cream.

6 Place in a very hot oven, 200°C/400°F/mark 6, until the top is a crisp golden brown.

Suggested wines

Tocai del Collio, Spumante Champenois del Trentino (Italy); Champagne (France); Californian Blanc de Blancs (U.S.A.); Rhine Sylvaner (Germany).

Gnocchi
Parisian style

Preparation: 50 minutes

225 ml/8 fl oz water
125 g/4 oz butter
salt
200 g/7 oz flour
4 eggs
nutmeg
150 ml/5 fl oz Mornay sauce
  (p. 179)

1 Bring the water and 80 g/3 oz butter to the boil in a high-sided saucepan. Add a pinch of salt.

2 When the butter has completely melted, remove from the heat and gradually add the flour, stirring constantly. Leave to cool slightly.

3 Beat in the eggs one at a time and add a pinch of nutmeg.

4 Spoon the mixture into a forcing bag with a 2.5-cm/1-in nozzle. Pipe gnocchi 4 cm/1½ in long into a saucepan of boiling salted water and cook for 15 minutes. Drain.

5 Heat the remaining butter in a small saucepan until light brown, then pour over the gnocchi.

6 Transfer the gnocchi to a lightly buttered ovenproof dish; cover with Mornay sauce and place in a very hot preheated oven, 200°C/400°F/mark 6, for 10 minutes until the top is golden brown.

Suggested wines

Ribolla dei Colli Orientali del Friuli, Pinot Grigio dell'Alto Adige (Italy); Pouilly Fuissé (France); Californian Chenin Blanc (U.S.A.); Rhine Sylvaner (Germany).

Tortelloni Bolognesi

Preparation: 1 hour 10 minutes

800 g/1¾ lb tortelloni
½ onion
350 g/12 oz ripe tomatoes
1 tbsp olive oil
salt, sugar
50 g/2 oz butter
4 tbsp grated Parmesan
black pepper

For the pasta
225 g/8 oz flour
2 egg yolks, 1 egg white

For the filling
1 egg, nutmeg
salt, black pepper
2 tbsp chopped fresh parsley
50 g/2 oz grated Parmesan
250 g/8 oz ricotta

Suggested wines

Tocai del Collio, Pinot dell'Oltrepò Pavese (Italy);
Meursault (France); Californian Chardonnay (U.S.A.);
Chenin Blanc (Australia).

1 Prepare the dough (p.180) with the flour and egg yolks and roll out a sheet of pasta. Using a pastry cutter cut into circles 7 cm/2¾ in in diameter.

2 Mix together in a bowl the egg, a pinch each of nutmeg, salt and pepper, the chopped parsley and Parmesan. Add the ricotta and stir until smooth and well blended.

3 Place a spoonful of filling in the centre of each circle. Brush the edges with egg white, fold in half and press firmly to seal.

4 Finely slice the onion.

5 Skin the tomatoes, discard the seeds and chop coarsely. Heat the olive oil in a large frying pan and fry the onion over moderate heat for 3 minutes before adding the tomatoes.

6 Cook for another 10 minutes, add salt, a pinch of sugar and the butter and cook for a further 15 minutes.

7 Cook the tortelloni in boiling salted water for 4–5 minutes. Drain well.

8 Serve in heated dishes with a sprinkling of grated Parmesan, freshly ground black pepper and a few spoonfuls of tomato sauce.

Semolina gnocchi

Preparation: 1 hour (+2 hours
for the semolina to stand)

500 ml/18 fl oz milk
100 g/3½ oz butter
salt
200 g/7 oz fine semolina
4 tbsp grated Parmesan
1 tbsp grated Sbrinz cheese

1 Heat the milk in a saucepan, add one-third of the butter and a pinch of salt.

2 Bring to the boil then gradually stir in the semolina. Cook for 20 minutes, stirring frequently.

3 Remove from the heat and stir in 2 tbsp grated Parmesan.

4 Pour the semolina into a dampened shallow dish, spreading it out evenly to a thickness of about 5 mm/¼ in.

5 Leave to cool for 2 hours then cut into circles 4 cm/1½ in in diameter.

6 Arrange the gnocchi slightly overlapping in a buttered ovenproof dish and sprinkle with the remaining Parmesan.

7 Melt the remaining butter and pour it over the gnocchi.

8 Cover with the grated Sbrinz and transfer to a very hot preheated oven, 200°C/400°F/ mark 6, for about 10 minutes until lightly browned.

Suggested wines

Orvieto, Soave (Italy); Pouilly Fumé (France); Californian Chardonnay (U.S.A.); Moselle Riesling (Germany).

Macaroni with eggs

Preparation: 20 minutes

275 g/10 oz macaroni
salt
40 g/1½ oz butter
2 eggs
1 egg yolk
2 tbsp chopped fresh parsley
4 tbsp grated Parmesan

1 Cook the macaroni in boiling salted water for 10–12 minutes until *al dente*. Drain well.

2 Melt the butter in a large frying pan; add the macaroni and stir gently.

3 In a small bowl beat the eggs and egg yolk with a pinch of salt, the parsley and half the Parmesan.

4 Pour the egg mixture over the macaroni and stir well over low heat for 30 seconds until the eggs begin to scramble.

5 Sprinkle with the remaining Parmesan and stir well before serving.

Suggested wines

Rosato del Salento, Terlano dell'Alto Adige (Italy); Rosé de Loire (France); Californian Chenin Blanc (U.S.A.); Chardonnay (South Africa).

Ham and cheese cannelloni

Preparation: 1 hour 10 minutes

800 g/1¾ lb cannelloni
salt
1 tbsp olive oil
For the sauce
40 g/1½ oz butter
40 g/1½ oz flour
300 ml/10 fl oz milk
white pepper

For the pasta
300 g/10 oz flour
3 eggs

For the filling
200 g/7 oz ricotta
3 tbsp grated Parmesan
125 g/4 oz cooked ham
salt, black pepper

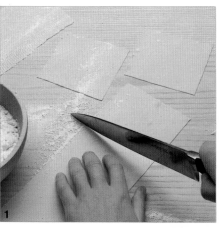
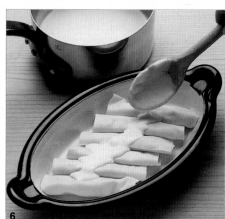

1 Prepare a sheet of pasta (p. 180) by combining the flour and eggs. Roll out very thinly and cut into 10-cm/4-in squares.

2 Cook in boiling salted water for 3–5 minutes with 1 tbsp olive oil to prevent them sticking. Drain carefully when *al dente* and spread out on a clean cloth.

3 Mix together in a bowl the ricotta, Parmesan, diced ham, salt and black pepper.

4 Place some of the filling on each square and roll up into cannelloni.

5 Melt the butter and stir in the flour. Gradually add the hot milk, then simmer for 10 minutes, stirring occasionally. Season with salt and white pepper.

6 Place the cannelloni in a buttered ovenproof dish. Cover with white sauce and place in a preheated oven, 170°C/325°F/ mark 3, for 8 minutes before serving.

Suggested wines

Montecarlo Bianco, Ribolla dei Colli Orientali del Friuli (Italy); Meursault (France); Californian Chenin Blanc (U.S.A.); Chardonnay (South Africa).

114

Maccheroncini with four cheeses

Preparation: 30 minutes

275 g/10 oz maccheroncini
salt
50 g/2 oz Gorgonzola cheese
50 g/2 oz Fontina cheese
50 g/2 oz Emmenthal cheese
2 tbsp butter
4 tbsp grated Parmesan
black pepper

1 Cook the maccheroncini in boiling salted water for 10–12 minutes until *al dente*.

2 Drain well and transfer to a buttered flameproof dish.

3 Dice the cheeses and sprinkle evenly over the top.

4 Place in a preheated oven, 170°C/325°F/mark 3, for 6 minutes.

5 Remove from the oven, add the butter and sprinkle with the grated Parmesan and plenty of freshly ground black pepper. Stir well for 2 minutes over high heat before serving.

Suggested wines

Pinot Spumante di Franciacorta, Greco di Tufo (Italy); Chassagne Montrachet (France); Californian Chenin Blanc (U.S.A.); Chardonnay (South Africa).

Maccheroncini with mascarpone

Preparation: 20 minutes

275 g/10 oz maccheroncini
salt
3 egg yolks (room temperature)
6 tbsp grated Parmesan
125 g/4 oz mascarpone (cream
   cheese)
black pepper
nutmeg

1 Cook the maccheroncini in boiling salted water for 10–12 minutes until *al dente*. Drain.

2 Mix the egg yolks with the grated Parmesan in a large, very hot tureen.

3 Place the tureen over a saucepan of boiling water so that it is heated by the steam.

4 Add the mascarpone, a generous sprinkling of freshly ground black pepper and a pinch of nutmeg. Stir well.

5 Pour in the very hot maccheroncini and mix well over heat before serving.

Suggested wines

Soave, Terlano dell'Alto Adige (Italy); Graves Blanc (France); Californian Chardonnay (U.S.A.); Chenin Blanc (South Africa).

Spinach and ricotta cannelloni

Preparation: 1 hour 10 minutes

3 eggs, salt
50 g/2 oz butter
300 ml/10 fl oz milk
125 g/4 oz flour

For the filling
350 g/12 oz spinach
225 g/8 oz ricotta

1 tbsp grated Parmesan
black pepper
salt

For the sauce
2–3 ripe tomatoes
1 sprig rosemary
salt
40 g/1½ oz butter
16 fresh basil leaves

Suggested wines

Orvieto, Lugana (Italy); Chablis (France); Californian Chardonnay (U.S.A.); Chenin Blanc (South Africa).

1 Prepare the cannelloni: beat the eggs in a bowl with a pinch of salt, 25 g/1 oz melted butter and the milk. Gradually beat in the flour until the mixture is smooth.

2 Melt a little butter in a 15-cm/6-in frying pan and pour in a few tablespoons of batter to cover the pan thinly.

3 Fry briefly on both sides over moderate heat. Make twelve cannelloni in all.

4 Rinse the spinach and cook over moderate heat with no extra water for 5–10 minutes or until tender. Drain well and chop finely. Mix together with the ricotta, grated Parmesan, freshly ground black pepper and salt.

5 Place a little of the filling mixture down the centre of each pancake and roll over to form cannelloni.

6 Dice the tomatoes and cook for 12 minutes in a small frying pan with a sprig of rosemary and a pinch of salt.

7 Push the tomatoes through a sieve with the back of a wooden spoon. Add the 40 g/1½ oz butter and 4 basil leaves and cook for 3 minutes in a small saucepan.

8 Place the cannelloni in a buttered ovenproof dish and transfer to a preheated oven, 170°C/325°F/mark 3, for 8 minutes. Serve in individual dishes with a few tablespoons of tomato sauce and garnished with more basil leaves.

119

Macaroni au gratin

Preparation: 30 minutes

275 g/10 oz macaroni
50 g/2 oz butter
40 g/1½ oz flour
300 ml/10 fl oz milk
white pepper
salt
4 tbsp grated Parmesan
2 egg yolks

1 Melt half the butter in a small saucepan. Stir in the flour, cook for 2 minutes, then gradually add the hot milk. Cook for 10 minutes, season with white pepper and keep hot.

2 Cook the macaroni in boiling salted water for 10–12 minutes until *al dente*. Drain well.

3 Return the white sauce to the heat; add the grated Parmesan, stir for 2 minutes, remove from the heat and stir in the egg yolks.

4 Pour the white sauce over the macaroni and mix well.

5 Transfer to a buttered ovenproof dish and place in a very hot preheated oven, 240°C/475°F/mark 9, for 8 minutes until golden brown on top.

6 Remove from the oven and serve in heated dishes.

Suggested wines

Tocai del Collio, Vernaccia di San Gimignano (Italy); Sancerre (France); Californian Sauvignon Blanc (U.S.A.); Chenin Blanc (South Africa).

Spaghetti with mild Pecorino cheese

Preparation: 20 minutes

275 g/10 oz spaghetti
salt
6 tbsp grated mild Pecorino
  cheese
black pepper

1 Cook the spaghetti in boiling salted water for 10–12 minutes or until *al dente*.

2 Drain the spaghetti, reserving a little of the cooking water, and transfer to a heated tureen.

3 Stir the grated Pecorino into the spaghetti and add a little of the cooking water to moisten if necessary.

4 Sprinkle generously with freshly ground black pepper, stir well and serve at once.

Suggested wines

Frascati, Lugana (Italy); Pouilly Fuissé (France); Californian Chardonnay (U.S.A.); Sauvignon Blanc (South Africa).

Tortelli
Piacenza style

Preparation: 1 hour 10 minutes

800 g/1¾ lb tortelli
salt
2 tbsp grated Parmesan
50 g/2 oz butter

For the pasta
300 g/10 oz flour
3 eggs

For the filling
400 g/14 oz spinach
1 egg
nutmeg
salt
black pepper
50 g/2 oz grated Parmesan
150 g/5 oz ricotta
125 g/4 oz mascarpone (cream
    cheese)

Suggested wines

Pinot Grigio dell'Alto Adige, Trebbiano di Romagna (Italy);
Bordeaux Blanc (France); Californian Chenin Blanc
(U.S.A.); Chardonnay (Australia).

1 Prepare the dough (p. 180); roll into a thin sheet and cut into diamond shapes with 8-cm/3-in sides.

2 Cook the spinach for 5–10 minutes in only the water remaining on the leaves after rinsing. When tender, drain well and chop coarsely.

3 Mix together in a small bowl with the egg, a pinch of nutmeg, salt and freshly ground black pepper.

4 Place a little of the filling mixture in the centre of each diamond.

5 Fold in half, press round the edges to seal then press the two outer points together to make tortelli.

6 Cook in boiling salted water for 2 minutes, then drain well.

7 Serve in individual heated dishes and sprinkle with grated Parmesan.

8 Melt the butter and spoon a little over each serving.

123

Fettuccine with butter

Preparation: 1 hour

400 g/14 oz fettuccine
salt
125 g/4 oz butter
125 g/4 oz grated Parmesan

For the pasta
250 g/9 oz flour
3 eggs
1 egg yolk
salt

1 Prepare the fettuccine (p. 181). Cook in boiling salted water for 3 minutes or until *al dente*.

2 Drain the fettuccine, reserving a little of the cooking water.

3 Place the butter in a large tureen over a saucepan of simmering water. When the butter has melted, add the fettuccine and the grated Parmesan.

4 Stir well, adding a little of the reserved cooking water if necessary. Serve without delay.

Suggested wines

Pinot Spumante del Trentino, Orvieto (Italy); Champagne (France); Californian Blanc de Blancs (U.S.A.); Blanc Fumé (South Africa).

Pasta spirals
Vesuvius style

Preparation: 30 minutes

275 g/10 oz pasta spirals
350 g/12 oz ripe tomatoes
6 tbsp olive oil
salt
black pepper
125 g/4 oz mozzarella
2 tbsp grated Pecorino cheese
oregano

1 Skin the tomatoes, discard the seeds and chop coarsely.

2 Heat the olive oil in a frying pan and cook the tomatoes for 10 minutes, adding a little salt.

3 Add a sprinkling of freshly ground black pepper, the thinly sliced mozzarella, grated Pecorino and a pinch of oregano.

4 Cover and cook for a further 4 minutes.

5 Cook the pasta spirals in plenty of boiling salted water for 10–12 minutes until *al dente*. Drain.

6 Pour the pasta into the frying pan and mix well. Transfer to a buttered ovenproof dish and place in a preheated oven, 180°C/350°F/mark 4, for 4 minutes before serving.

Suggested wines

Ischia Bianco, Vernaccia di San Gimignano (Italy); Graves Blanc (France); Californian Chenin Blanc (U.S.A.); Sauvignon Blanc (South Africa).

Spinach tagliatelle with cheese

Preparation: 1 hour (+1 hour for the cheeses to stand)

350 g/12 oz spinach tagliatelle
125 g/4 oz Emmenthal cheese
125 g/4 oz Fontina cheese
125 ml/4 fl oz milk
25 g/1 oz butter
1 egg yolk

salt
2 tbsp grated Parmesan
black pepper

For the pasta
300 g/10 oz flour
225 g/8 oz spinach
3 eggs
salt

1 Cut the cheeses into small dice. Place in a large frying pan with the milk and butter and leave for 1 hour.

2 Place the frying pan over moderate heat to melt the diced cheese. Beat in the egg yolk with a whisk and continue stirring for 3 minutes.

3 Put the tagliatelle (p. 181) in a large saucepan of boiling salted water and cook for 3 minutes if fresh, 6 minutes if dried. Drain.

4 Pour into the frying pan with the cheeses, sprinkle with grated Parmesan and mix carefully. Sprinkle with pepper and serve at once.

Suggested wines

Lugana, Torgiano Bianco (Italy); Pouilly Fuissé (France); Californian Pinot Blanc (U.S.A.); Müller Thurgau (New Zealand).

Pasta with fish and seafood

Spaghettini with clams

Preparation: 30 minutes (+2 hours to clean the clams)

275 g/10 oz spaghettini
800 g/1¾ lb clams
salt
6 tbsp olive oil
1 clove garlic
black pepper
1 tbsp chopped fresh parsley

1 Leave the clams to soak under cold running water for 2 hours to remove all traces of sand.

2 Drain and heat in a large covered saucepan for about 4 minutes.

3 Remove the clams from their shells. Strain the cooking liquor and reduce in a small saucepan over high heat for 2–3 minutes.

4 Cook the spaghettini in boiling salted water for 8–10 minutes. Drain.

5 Heat the olive oil in a large frying pan and fry the finely chopped garlic for 30 seconds over low heat.

6 Add the clams and spaghettini and the reduced cooking liquor. Stir for 1 minute over moderate heat; sprinkle with freshly ground black pepper and chopped parsley and serve at once.

Suggested wines

Ischia Bianco, Regaleali Bianco (Italy); Chablis (France); Californian Pinot Blanc (U.S.A.); Chardonnay (Australia).

Chilled spaghettini with caviar

Preparation: 20 minutes

225 g/8 oz spaghettini
salt
4 tbsp olive oil
1 tbsp finely chopped fresh
  chives
4 tbsp caviar

1 Cook the spaghettini in boiling salted water for 8–10 minutes until *al dente*. Drain.

2 Leave to stand under cold running water in a colander for at least 1 minute.

3 Pour into a large bowl, add the olive oil and chopped chives and mix well.

4 Serve in individual dishes, each portion garnished with a spoonful of caviar.

Suggested wines

Pinot Spumante di Franciacorta, Sauvignon del Collio (Italy); Champagne (France); Californian Blanc de Blancs (U.S.A.); Chardonnay (Australia).

Seafood spaghettini

Preparation: 50 minutes (+2
hours to clean the molluscs)

225 g/8 oz spaghettini
1 kg/2 lb assorted molluscs
   (mussels, clams, sea dates)
4 jumbo prawns
salt
6 tbsp olive oil

1 ripe tomato
1 clove garlic
1 tbsp chopped fresh parsley
black pepper

1 Leave the molluscs to stand in a colander under cold running water for 2 hours to remove all traces of sand. Drain and place in a large frying pan. Cover and heat for 3 minutes until the shells open.

2 Remove the meat from the shells. Reserve and strain the cooking liquor.

3 Steam the jumbo prawns or cook in salted water for 4 minutes.

4 Pour 5 tbsp olive oil into a large frying pan. Skin, seed and chop the tomato and add to the oil. Cook for 5 minutes then add the molluscs, prawns and reserved liquor.

5 Pour 1 tbsp oil into a small frying pan, add the finely chopped garlic and cook over low heat for 2 minutes.

6 Cook the spaghettini in boiling salted water for 8–10 minutes until *al dente*. Drain and pour into the frying pan with the tomato sauce and molluscs. Sprinkle with freshly ground black pepper, chopped parsley and the garlic-flavoured oil. Mix well before serving.

Suggested wines

Torbato, Trebbiano di Romagna (Italy); Pouilly Fuissé (France); Vinho Verde (Portugal); Chardonnay (New Zealand).

Spaghettini with mullet roe

Preparation: 20 minutes

275 g/10 oz spaghettini
salt
6 tbsp olive oil
2 cloves garlic
¼ red chilli pepper
125 g/4 oz mullet roe

1 Cook the spaghettini in boiling salted water for 8–10 minutes until *al dente*.

2 Heat the olive oil in a frying pan; add the finely chopped garlic and thinly sliced chilli pepper and fry gently over low heat for 2–3 minutes.

3 Carefully peel off the thin skin surrounding the mullet roe. Grate the roe.

4 Pour the drained spaghettini into the frying pan with the garlic and chilli pepper and heat gently for 2 minutes.

5 Serve in individual heated dishes and sprinkle with the grated mullet roe.

Suggested wines

Terlano, Pinot Spumante dell'Oltrepò Pavese (Italy); Champagne (France); Californian Blanc de Blancs (U.S.A.); Chenin Blanc (Australia).

Tagliolini
with scallops

Preparation: 1 hour

275 g/10 oz tagliolini
25 g/1 oz butter
275 g/10 oz shelled scallops
6 tbsp white wine
salt
6 tbsp single cream
4 fresh basil leaves

½ tsp chopped fresh chives
black pepper

For the pasta
200 g/7 oz flour
2 eggs
salt

1 Melt the butter in a frying pan. Add the rinsed and dried scallops, sprinkle with white wine and a little salt; cover and cook for 5 minutes.

2 Remove the scallops with a slotted spoon and keep warm.

3 Pour the cream into the frying pan; add the finely chopped basil and chopped chives and cook for 2 minutes until slightly reduced.

4 Slice the scallops thinly, add to the frying pan and cook for 1 minute.

5 Cook the tagliolini (p. 181) in boiling salted water for 3–4 minutes until *al dente*. Drain.

6 Pour into the frying pan with the scallops. Sprinkle with freshly ground black pepper and mix well over high heat for 2 minutes before serving.

Suggested wines

Tocai del Collio, Torgiano Bianco (Italy); Bourgogne Blanc (France); Californian Chenin Blanc (U.S.A.); Müller Thurgau (New Zealand).

Penne with clams and peas

Preparation: 40 minutes (+2 hours to clean the clams)

275 g/10 oz fluted penne
400 g/14 oz clams
400 g/14 oz peas
6 tbsp olive oil
salt
1 tbsp chopped fresh parsley
black pepper

1 Leave the clams in a colander under cold running water for 2 hours to remove all traces of sand.

2 Drain and heat for 2–3 minutes in a large covered frying pan over high heat until the shells open.

3 Remove the clams from their shells. Strain and reserve the cooking liquor.

4 Shell the peas and simmer for 12 minutes in a large frying pan with the olive oil and 125 ml/4 fl oz of the reserved liquor. Season with salt.

5 Cook the penne in boiling salted water for 10–12 minutes until *al dente*. Drain.

6 Add the clams to the peas and cook for a further 2 minutes. Add salt if necessary. Pour in the penne, sprinkle with chopped parsley and black pepper and mix well for 1 minute before serving.

Suggested wines

Soave, Frascati (Italy); Bordeaux Blanc (France); Californian Chenin Blanc (U.S.A.); Müller Thurgau (Germany).

Tagliolini with seafood and sweet peppers

Preparation: 1 hour (+2 hours for cleaning the molluscs)

275 g/10 oz tagliolini
600 g/1¼ lb assorted molluscs (clams, mussels, sea dates)
¼ sweet yellow pepper
¼ sweet red pepper

6 tbsp olive oil
salt
black pepper

For the pasta
200 g/7 oz flour
2 eggs
salt

1 Leave the molluscs to stand under cold running water for at least 2 hours, stirring frequently.

2 Drain well and place in a large frying pan. Cover and cook for 2–3 minutes over high heat until the shells open.

3 Remove from their shells. Strain and reserve the cooking liquor.

4 Cut the peppers into thin strips. Heat 5 tbsp olive oil in a large frying pan, add the peppers and cook for about 12 minutes or until tender. Add a few tablespoons water if necessary.

5 Cook the tagliolini (p. 181) in boiling salted water for 3–4 minutes until *al dente*. Drain.

6 Add the molluscs and reserved cooking liquor to the peppers and cook for 2–3 minutes. Pour in the tagliolini, 1 tbsp oil and sprinkle with freshly ground black pepper. Mix well for 2 minutes over high heat before serving.

Suggested wines

Sauvignon del Collio, Sylvaner dell'Alto Adige (Italy); Montrachet (France); Californian Gewürztraminer (U.S.A.); Chardonnay (South Africa).

Ditalini with mussels and jumbo prawns

Preparation: 40 minutes (+2
  hours to clean the mussels)

275 g/10 oz ditalini
400 g/14 oz mussels
125 g/4 oz jumbo prawns
salt
6 tbsp olive oil

1 clove garlic
1 tbsp chopped fresh parsley
black pepper

Suggested wines

Soave, Vermentino (Italy); Chablis (France); Californian
Chenin Blanc (U.S.A.); Müller Thurgau (New Zealand).

1 Leave the mussels under cold running water for 2 hours to get rid of all traces of sand. Drain, then place in a covered frying pan over high heat for 3 minutes until the shells open. Shake the pan occasionally.

2 Remove the mussels from their shells and strain the liquor.

3 Steam the peeled jumbo prawns for 4 minutes.

4 Reduce the reserved cooking liquor over high heat in a small frying pan then add the mussels and prawns.

5 Cook the ditalini in boiling salted water for 10–12 minutes until *al dente*.

6 Heat the olive oil in a large frying pan and lightly brown the finely diced garlic. Add the ditalini and stir briefly.

7 Pour the mussels and prawns into the ditalini.

8 Sprinkle with chopped parsley, salt and freshly ground black pepper and stir for 1 minute over high heat before serving.

Maccheroncini with mussels

Preparation: 30 minutes (+2
  hours to clean the mussels)

275 g/10 oz maccheroncini
1 kg/2 lb mussels
1 clove garlic
6 tbsp olive oil
1 tbsp chopped fresh parsley

1–2 large ripe tomatoes
salt
black pepper

1 Leave the mussels under cold running water for 2 hours to remove all traces of sand.

2 Drain well, then place in a covered frying pan over high heat for 3 minutes until the shells open. Shake the frying pan occasionally.

3 Remove the mussels from their shells and keep warm.

4 Finely dice the garlic and heat for 2 minutes in the olive oil in a large frying pan. Add the parsley and the skinned, seeded and chopped tomatoes.

5 Sprinkle with salt and cook for 8 minutes. Add the mussels.

6 Cook the maccheroncini in boiling salted water for 10–12 minutes until *al dente*. Drain.

7 Pour the maccheroncini into the frying pan, sprinkle with freshly ground black pepper and stir for 1 minute over high heat before serving.

Suggested wines

Corvo di Salaparuta, Martinafranca (Italy); Graves Blanc (France); Californian Chenin Blanc (U.S.A.); Rhine Riesling (Germany).

Penne with tuna

Preparation: 20 minutes

275 g/10 oz penne
1 onion
5 tbsp olive oil
salt
200 g/7 oz canned tuna
1 tbsp chopped fresh parsley
black pepper

1 Finely slice the onion.

2 Heat the olive oil in a large frying pan; add the onion, sprinkle with salt and cook for 3 minutes. Add 125 ml/4 fl oz water and cook for a further 5 minutes.

3 Add the drained and flaked tuna and cook for 3 minutes.

4 Meanwhile, cook the penne in boiling salted water for 10–12 minutes until *al dente*. Drain.

5 Pour the penne into the frying pan. Sprinkle with chopped parsley and freshly ground black pepper.

6 Stir over high heat for 1 minute before serving.

Suggested wines

Greco di Tufo, Ribolla dei Colli Orientali del Friuli (Italy); Meursault (France); Californian Chenin Blanc (U.S.A.); Müller Thurgau (Germany).

Seafood pasta squares

Preparation: 1 hour 10 minutes (+2 hours to clean the clams)

8 pasta squares
350 g/12 oz clams
225 g/8 oz shelled scallops
175 ml/6 fl oz olive oil
2 cloves garlic
salt

6 tbsp white wine
pepper
30 fresh basil leaves
10 pine nuts

For the pasta
200 g/7 oz flour
2 eggs
salt

1 Prepare and roll out a thin sheet of pasta (p. 180) and cut into eight 12-cm/5-in squares.

2 Leave the clams under cold running water for 2 hours to remove all traces of sand. Drain and place in a covered frying pan over high heat for 2–3 minutes until the shells open. Remove from their shells and keep warm.

3 Clean the scallops and discard the black muscle attached to each one.

4 Pour 3 tbsp olive oil into a frying pan; add 1 finely sliced clove of garlic and fry for 1 minute. Add the scallops; sprinkle with salt and add the white wine. Stir and cook for 6 minutes. Add the clams, sprinkle with pepper and cook for a further 2 minutes.

5 Place a clove of garlic, 30 basil leaves, the pine nuts, a pinch of salt and 125 ml/4 fl oz olive oil in a mortar and pound to a smooth paste.

6 Cook the squares of pasta in boiling salted water for 3–5 minutes, adding 1 tbsp oil to prevent them sticking together. Drain well and place one pasta square on each heated plate. Spoon some of the seafood on top with a little of the basil sauce. Cover with a second pasta square and a trickle of basil sauce.

Suggested wines

Gavi, Bianchello del Metauro (Italy); Chablis (France); Californian Chardonnay (U.S.A.); Rhine Sylvaner (Germany).

Fettuccine with smoked salmon

Preparation: 20 minutes

275 g/10 oz fettuccine
125 g/4 oz smoked salmon
25 g/1 oz butter
175 ml/6 fl oz single cream
salt
white pepper
1 tbsp caviar
½ tsp chopped fresh chives

1 Cut the salmon into 1-cm/ ½-in dice.

2 Melt the butter in a large frying pan; add the cream and a pinch of salt and cook for a few minutes until slightly reduced.

3 Add the smoked salmon and heat for 3 minutes.

4 Cook the fettuccine in boiling salted water for 6 minutes until *al dente*. Drain.

5 Pour the fettuccine into the frying pan. Sprinkle with pepper and stir over high heat for 2 minutes.

6 Serve in individual dishes and garnish with a little caviar and chopped chives.

Suggested wines

Spumante Champenois del Trentino, Pinot dell'Oltrepò Pavese (Italy); Pouilly Fumé (France); Californian Gewürztraminer (U.S.A.); Rhine Riesling (Germany).

Spaghettini with lobster

Preparation: 1 hour

275 g/10 oz spaghettini
1 small lobster (450 g/1 lb)
salt
½ onion
4 tbsp olive oil
2 small ripe tomatoes
1 sprig fresh rosemary
black pepper

1 Plunge the lobster into boiling salted water for 8 minutes. Leave to cool slightly then cut in half.

2 Remove the meat from the tail and claws and cut into pieces.

3 Chop the onion finely and cook for a few minutes in the olive oil and an equal quantity of water. Add the skinned, seeded and chopped tomatoes and the rosemary. Sprinkle with salt and cook for 5 minutes.

4 Sieve the tomato sauce and pour into a large frying pan.

5 Add the pieces of lobster, adjust the seasoning and cook for 3 minutes.

6 Cook the spaghettini in boiling salted water for 8–10 minutes until *al dente*. Drain and pour into the frying pan. Sprinkle with pepper and stir briefly over moderate heat before serving.

Suggested wines

Pinot Champenois del Trentino, Pinot di Franciacorta (Italy); Champagne (France); Californian Blanc de Blancs (U.S.A.); Rhine Sylvaner (Germany).

Spaghettini with baby cuttlefish

Preparation: 50 minutes

275 g/10 oz spaghettini
350 g/12 oz baby cuttlefish
½ small onion
125 ml/4 fl oz olive oil
salt
1 large ripe tomato

1 sprig fresh rosemary
black pepper
sprigs fresh parsley

Suggested wines

Tocai del Collio, Verdicchio dei Castelli di Jesi (Italy);
Pouilly Fuissé (France); Californian Chenin Blanc (U.S.A.);
Rhine Sylvaner (Germany).

144

1 Pull away the ink sac from the cuttlefish and reserve the ink. Rinse and dry the cuttlefish and remove the hard inner bone.

2 Finely slice the onion.

3 Heat half the olive oil in a frying pan, add the onion and fry until transparent. Add the cuttlefish, sprinkle with salt and cook for 3 minutes.

4 Add the skinned, seeded and chopped tomato and the sprig of rosemary. Stir and cook for 10 minutes.

5 Remove the cuttlefish and keep warm.

6 Add the reserved ink to the sauce and cook for 4 minutes.

7 Sieve the tomato sauce, pour into a large frying pan and add the remaining oil. Cook for 2 minutes.

8 Cook the spaghettini in boiling salted water for 8–10 minutes until *al dente*. Drain. Pour into the sauce, sprinkle with freshly ground black pepper and mix well. Serve on individual plates and spoon the cuttlefish on top. Garnish with sprigs of parsley.

Spaghettini with scampi and clams

Preparation: 40 minutes (+2
    hours to clean the clams)

225 g/8 oz spaghettini
450 g/1 lb clams
12 scampi
salt
1 clove garlic
125 ml/4 fl oz olive oil

black pepper
1 tbsp chopped fresh parsley
1 tbsp chopped fresh basil

1 Leave the clams under cold running water for 2 hours.

2 Drain and place in a covered frying pan over high heat for 2–3 minutes until the shells open.

3 Remove from their shells. Strain and reserve the liquor.

4 Steam the scampi or cook in a little boiling salted water for 4 minutes. Peel them; remove the grey matter from the head and place it in a frying pan with the reserved liquor.

5 Finely dice the garlic and brown lightly in the olive oil over low heat for 2 minutes.

Strain and pour into the frying pan with the liquor. Add the clams and the scampi and heat for 2 minutes.

6 Cook the spaghettini in boiling salted water for 8–10 minutes until *al dente*. Drain and add to the frying pan. Sprinkle with freshly ground black pepper, chopped parsley and basil and heat for 2 minutes before serving.

Suggested wines

Verdicchio dei Castelli di Jesi, Riesling Renano dei Colli Orientali del Friuli (Italy); Sancerre (France); Californian Sauvignon Blanc (U.S.A.); Rhine Riesling (Germany).

Tagliolini
with razor clams

Preparation: 1 hour (+2 hours
to clean the clams)

275 g/10 oz tagliolini
600 g/1¼ lb small razor clams
salt
6 tbsp olive oil
1 clove garlic
1 tbsp chopped fresh parsley
black pepper

For the pasta
200 g/7 oz flour
2 eggs
salt

1 Leave the clams under cold running water for 2 hours.

2 Drain and place in a covered frying pan for 3 minutes over high heat until the shells open.

3 Remove from their shells, discarding the heads, and rinse to remove all traces of sand. Strain and reserve the cooking liquor.

4 Cook the tagliolini (p. 181) in boiling salted water for 3–4 minutes until *al dente*. Drain.

5 Reduce the liquor over high heat in a large frying pan. Add the clams and tagliolini, sprinkle with salt and cook for 2 minutes.

6 Heat the olive oil in a small saucepan and lightly brown the finely diced garlic. Strain and pour over the tagliolini. Mix well, sprinkle with chopped parsley and pepper and serve at once.

Suggested wines

Gavi, Lugana (Italy); Bourgogne Blanc (France); Californian Chardonnay (U.S.A.); Müller Thurgau (Germany).

Tagliatelle with scallops

Preparation: 1 hour 10 minutes

275 g/10 oz tagliatelle
1 leek
50 g/2 oz butter
salt
175 g/6 oz shelled scallops
6 tbsp white wine
black pepper

For the pasta
200 g/7 oz flour
2 eggs
salt

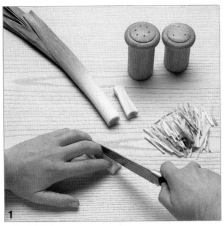

1 Wash the leek thoroughly and cut into matchstick strips. Rinse again.

2 Melt half the butter in a frying pan; add the leek and 6 tbsp water, sprinkle with salt and cook for 8 minutes.

3 Melt the remaining butter in a separate frying pan. Add the scallops and white wine. Sprinkle with salt, cover and cook gently for 5 minutes.

4 Remove the scallops with a slotted spoon and slice thinly.

5 Pour the cooking juices into the frying pan with the leek and cook for 2 minutes.

6 Cook the tagliatelle (p. 181) in boiling salted water for 3 minutes until *al dente*. Drain and pour into the frying pan. Sprinkle with black pepper and stir over high heat for 2 minutes before serving.

Suggested wines

Ribolla dei Colli Orientali del Friuli, Frascati (Italy); Pinot d'Alsace (France); Californian Chenin Blanc (U.S.A.); Müller Thurgau (Germany).

148

Wholewheat spaghetti with anchovies

Preparation: 30 minutes

275 g/10 oz wholewheat
  spaghetti
1 onion
125 ml/4 fl oz olive oil
salt
80 g/3 oz salted anchovies
black pepper

1 Finely chop the onion.

2 Pour half the olive oil into a large frying pan. Add the onion and cook for 2 minutes. Sprinkle with salt, add 125 ml/ 4 fl oz water and cook for a further 5 minutes.

3 Rinse and bone the anchovies, then chop finely.

4 Add to the onion and cook for 4 minutes. Pour in the remaining oil.

5 Cook the spaghetti in boiling salted water for 12–15 minutes until *al dente*. Drain.

6 Pour the spaghetti into the frying pan; sprinkle with freshly ground black pepper and mix well over high heat before serving.

Suggested wines

Frascati, Corvo di Salaparuta (Italy); Pinot d'Alsace (France); Californian Johannisberg Riesling (U.S.A.); Rhine Riesling (Germany).

Spaghettini with olives, anchovies and capers

Preparation: 40 minutes

275 g/10 oz spaghettini
50 g/2 oz salted anchovies
6 tbsp olive oil
1 clove garlic
½ red chilli pepper
2 large ripe tomatoes

50 g/2 oz pitted black olives
30 capers
salt
black pepper

1 Rinse and bone the anchovies.

2 Pour the olive oil into a large frying pan. Add the finely diced garlic and thinly sliced chilli pepper and fry gently for a few minutes. Add the chopped anchovies.

3 Simmer for 2 minutes then add the skinned, seeded and chopped tomatoes. Cook for 10 minutes.

4 Add the olives and capers, season and simmer for another 5 minutes.

5 Cook the spaghettini in boiling salted water for 8–10 minutes until *al dente*. Drain.

6 Pour the spaghettini into the frying pan and stir well before serving.

Suggested wines

Ischia Bianco, Verdicchio dei Castelli di Jesi (Italy); Chablis (France); Californian Chardonnay (U.S.A.); Rhine Riesling (Germany).

Cannelloni with pike and mushrooms

Preparation: 1 hour 20 minutes

800 g/1¾ lb cannelloni
salt
1 tbsp olive oil
40 g/1½ oz butter
1 shallot
pinch thyme
225 ml/8 fl oz single cream
black pepper

For the pasta
300 g/10 oz flour
3 eggs, salt
For the filling
350 g/12 oz pike, salt
40 g/1½ oz butter
4 tbsp white wine
2 tbsp olive oil
1 clove garlic
125 g/4 oz mushrooms

Suggested wines

Riesling dell'Oltrepò Pavese, Bianchello del Metauro (Italy);
Graves Blanc (France); Californian Chenin Blanc (U.S.A.);
Moselle Riesling (Germany).

1 Prepare a sheet of pasta by combining the flour, eggs and a pinch of salt (p. 180). Roll out and cut into 10-cm/4-in squares.

2 Clean and rinse the pike. Sprinkle with salt and place in a buttered ovenproof dish. Cover with the remaining butter, sprinkle with the white wine and place in a preheated oven, 180°C/350°F/mark 4, for 12 minutes.

3 Pour the olive oil into a small saucepan and lightly brown the finely sliced garlic. Add the cleaned and chopped mushrooms, sprinkle with salt and simmer for 4 minutes. Add 1 tbsp water and discard the garlic.

4 Cook the squares of pasta in boiling salted water for 3–5 minutes with 1 tbsp oil to prevent them sticking together. Drain and leave to dry on a clean cloth.

5 Place a little flaked fish and a spoonful of mushrooms on each square.

6 Roll up to make cannelloni and brush the edge with water. Press to seal.

7 Butter an ovenproof dish and arrange the cannelloni, sealed side down, in a single layer. Add a few flakes of butter and place in the oven at 180°C/350°F/mark 4 for 10 minutes.

8 Meanwhile, mix together in a blender the shallot, a pinch of thyme and the cream. Pour into a small saucepan and simmer for 3 minutes. Spoon the sauce over the cannelloni before serving.

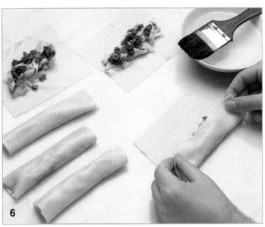

153

Pennette with scallops

Preparation: 20 minutes

275 g/10 oz pennette
350 g/12 oz shelled scallops
40 g/1½ oz butter
6 tbsp white wine
salt
1 tsp curry powder
125 ml/4 fl oz single cream
black pepper

1 Clean the scallops, removing the black muscle attached to each one.

2 Rinse and drain.

3 Melt the butter in a large frying pan. Add the scallops; pour in the wine, sprinkle with salt and cook for 6 minutes, stirring frequently.

4 Mix the curry powder with the warmed cream and pour into the frying pan. Cook for a further 3 minutes.

5 Meanwhile, cook the pennette in boiling salted water for 8–10 minutes until *al dente*. Drain.

6 Pour the pennette into the frying pan. Sprinkle with freshly ground black pepper and mix thoroughly over high heat before serving.

Suggested wines

Pinot di Franciacorta, Lugana (Italy); Chablis (France); Californian Sauvignon Blanc (U.S.A.); Rhine Sylvaner (Germany).

Pasta spirals with mussels and potatoes

Preparation: 40 minutes (+2 hours to clean the mussels)

225 g/8 oz pasta spirals
450 g/1 lb mussels
225 g/8 oz potatoes
salt

125 ml/4 fl oz olive oil
black pepper
1 tbsp chopped fresh parsley

1 Leave the mussels for 2 hours under cold running water.

2 Drain well and place in a large covered frying pan over high heat for 3 minutes until the shells open.

3 Remove the mussels from their shells. Strain and reserve the liquor.

4 Peel and slice the potatoes and cut into pieces.

5 Boil in salted water for 5–8 minutes or until tender. Drain.

6 Heat the olive oil in a large frying pan. Add the mussels and potatoes and cook for 2 minutes. Add 6 tbsp of the reserved liquor.

7 Cook the pasta spirals in boiling salted water for 10–12 minutes until *al dente*.

8 Drain and pour into the frying pan; sprinkle with pepper and chopped parsley and stir for a further 1 minute before serving.

Suggested wines

Martinafranca Bianco, Vernaccia di San Gimignano (Italy); Bourgogne Blanc (France); Californian Pinot Blanc (U.S.A.); Moselle Riesling (Germany).

Chilled spaghettini with raw salmon

Preparation: 30 minutes (+1 hour to marinate the salmon)

175 g/6 oz spaghettini
250 g/9 oz salmon steak
salt
2 tbsp lemon juice
5 tbsp olive oil
2 tbsp white wine
black pepper
pinch fresh wild fennel seeds
1 sprig fresh rosemary
1 clove garlic

1 Remove the skin and bone from the salmon steak and cut into small dice.

2 Place in a small bowl, sprinkle with salt, the lemon juice, 2 tbsp olive oil, the white wine, freshly ground black pepper and finely chopped fennel seeds. Leave to marinate for 1 hour.

3 Pour the remaining oil into a frying pan; add the rosemary and the quartered garlic and fry gently for 3 minutes.

4 Cook the spaghettini in boiling salted water for 8–10 minutes until *al dente*. Drain and leave under cold running water for 1 minute.

5 Discard the rosemary and garlic and pour the spaghettini into the frying pan. Turn off the heat and turn the spaghettini in the flavoured oil for a few seconds. Sprinkle with more freshly ground black pepper.

6 Serve in individual dishes with the marinated salmon on top.

This dish can also be served hot. If preferred, keep the spaghettini hot after draining and place the frying pan over the heat when turning the pasta in the flavoured oil.

Suggested wines

Pinot Champenois dell'Oltrepò Pavese, Pinot Grigio dell'Alto Adige (Italy); Champagne (France); Californian Blanc de Blancs (U.S.A.); Rhine Sylvaner (Germany).

Cannelloni
with lobster

Preparation: 1½ hours

8 cannelloni, salt
1 tbsp olive oil
25 g/1 oz butter
8 marrow flowers
6 tbsp single cream
pinch thyme, pepper
For the pasta
300 g/10 oz flour

3 eggs, salt
For the filling
1 lobster (450 g/1 lb)
25 g/1 oz butter
1 tbsp chopped onion
1 sprig fresh rosemary
1 ripe tomato, salt
4 tbsp single cream, pepper
25 g/1 oz fresh breadcrumbs
150 ml/5 fl oz milk

Suggested wines

Pinot Grigio dell'Alto Adige, Ribolla dei Colli Orientali del
Friuli (Italy); Pouilly Fuissé (France); Californian Blanc de
Blancs (U.S.A.); Moselle Riesling (Germany).

1 Prepare and roll out a thin sheet of pasta (p. 180) by combining the flour, eggs and a pinch of salt. Cut into eight 10-cm/4-in squares. Cook in boiling salted water for 3–5 minutes with 1 tbsp olive oil to prevent them sticking together. Drain and lay out on a clean cloth to dry.

2 Plunge the lobster into boiling salted water and cook for 8 minutes. Drain and cut in half; remove the meat from the shell and cut half into small dice. Cut the other half into larger pieces.

3 Melt the butter in a frying pan; add the chopped onion and a sprig of rosemary and fry gently for 2 minutes. Add the skinned, seeded and chopped tomato.

4 Cook for 4 minutes; sprinkle with salt and add the larger pieces of lobster. Pour in the cream and cook for 4 minutes.

5 Pour into a liquidizer, sprinkle with pepper and blend until smooth. Pour into a bowl and add the diced lobster and the fresh breadcrumbs, soaked in milk and squeezed. Stir well.

6 Place a little of the lobster mixture on each square of pasta and roll up to make cannelloni. Brush the edge with water to seal. Place in a buttered ovenproof dish and transfer to a preheated oven, 180°C/350°F/mark 4, for 10 minutes.

7 Meanwhile, rinse and dry the marrow flowers and fry gently in the butter for 4 minutes. Sprinkle with salt.

8 Add the cream, a pinch of thyme and a little pepper and cook for another 2 minutes. Liquidize briefly in a blender, then reheat before spooning the sauce over the cannelloni.

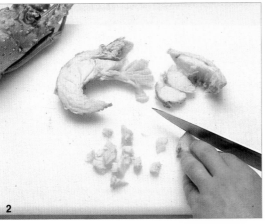

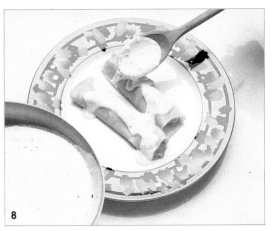

Pasta shells with mussels and turnip tops

Preparation: 40 minutes (+2 hours to clean the mussels)

225 g/8 oz pasta shells
400 g/14 oz mussels
225 g/8 oz turnip tops
salt
6 tbsp olive oil
1 clove garlic
pinch saffron threads

1 Leave the mussels under cold running water for 2 hours, stirring frequently to remove all traces of sand.

2 Drain and place in a covered frying pan over high heat for 3 minutes until the shells open.

3 Remove the mussels from their shells and keep warm.

4 Cook the turnip tops in salted water for 5–10 minutes until tender. Drain.

5 Heat the olive oil in a large frying pan and brown the sliced garlic for 2 minutes. Discard the garlic, then add the turnip tops, cut into small pieces. After 2 minutes add the mussels and the saffron soaked in 2 tbsp warm water. Cook for a few minutes more.

6 Cook the pasta shells in boiling salted water for 10–12 minutes until *al dente*.

7 Drain and add to the frying pan. Stir for 1 minute before serving.

Suggested wines

Corvo di Salaparuta, Torbato (Italy); Gewürztraminer d'Alsace (France); Californian Sauvignon Blanc (U.S.A.); Müller Thurgau (New Zealand).

Tagliatelle with sole and saffron

Preparation: 1 hour 10 minutes

275 g/10 oz fresh tagliatelle
275 g/10 oz sole fillet
50 g/2 oz butter
4 fresh chives
salt
2 tbsp white wine
6 tbsp fish fumet

pinch saffron threads
black pepper

For the pasta
200 g/7 oz flour
2 eggs
salt

1 Rinse and dry the sole and cut into thin strips.

2 Melt half the butter in a large frying pan. Add the chives and sole; sprinkle with salt, pour in the white wine, then cover and simmer for 4 minutes.

3 Heat the fumet and add the saffron threads.

4 Pour the fumet into the frying pan and simmer for a further 2 minutes. Discard the chives, add the remaining butter and simmer for a further 2 minutes.

5 Cook the tagliatelle (p. 181) in boiling salted water for 3 minutes until *al dente*. Drain.

6 Pour the tagliatelle into the frying pan. Sprinkle with pepper and mix carefully before serving.

Suggested wines

Pinot Champenois di Franciacorta, Ribolla dei Colli Orientali del Friuli (Italy); Gewürztraminer d'Alsace (France); Californian Johannisberg Riesling (U.S.A.); Rhine Riesling (Germany).

Open lasagne with scallops

Preparation: 1 hour 40 minutes

25 g/1 oz fresh egg pasta
4 spinach lasagne
4 large parsley leaves
400 g/14 oz shelled scallops
salt
black pepper

1 piece root ginger
125 g/4 oz butter
2 tbsp white wine
1 tbsp olive oil

Suggested wines

Pinot di Franciacorta, Greco di Tufo (Italy); Meursault (France); Californian Chardonnay (U.S.A.); Moselle Riesling (Germany).

1 Prepare the egg pasta (p. 180) and spinach lasagne (p. 182). Roll out the egg pasta very thinly and cut out eight squares. Place a parsley leaf in the centre of four squares; cover each with another thin square of lasagne and roll over with the rolling pin.

2 Cut the scallops in half; season with salt and freshly ground black pepper.

3 Peel the ginger; grate finely, then press with the back of a teaspoon until you have 1 tsp ginger juice.

4 Melt 25 g/1 oz butter in a frying pan and sauté the scallops briefly.

5 Pour in the white wine, simmer for 2–3 minutes then remove the scallops. Reduce the cooking liquor by boiling fast; add the ginger juice and the remaining butter, beating lightly with a whisk.

6 Cook both types of lasagne in plenty of boiling salted water for 3–5 minutes, adding 1 tbsp olive oil to prevent them sticking.

7 Drain and place a sheet of spinach lasagne on each plate.

8 Return the scallops to the frying pan to heat through, then pour over the spinch lasagne. Cover with the sheets of egg lasagne and serve without delay.

163

Maccheroncini with sardines

Preparation: 1 hour (+30 minutes to soak the sultanas)

275 g/10 oz maccheroncini
2 tbsp sultanas
salt
325 g/12 oz fresh sardines
6 tbsp olive oil

1 onion
2 tbsp freshly made tomato sauce
25 g/1 oz pine nuts
black pepper
2 anchovies

1 Soak the sultanas in warm water for 30 minutes.

2 Gut the sardines and remove the heads. Rinse and dry carefully.

3 Heat the olive oil in a large frying pan and fry the finely sliced onion gently. Add the freshly made tomato sauce, the pine nuts and the drained sultanas.

4 Cook for a further 5 minutes then add the sardines, salt and a sprinkling of freshly ground black pepper. Cover and cook for 10–12 minutes.

5 Add the rinsed and finely chopped anchovies and cook for another 5 minutes.

6 Boil the maccheroncini for 10–12 minutes. Drain when *al dente* and add to the frying pan with the sardines. Leave to stand for 3 minutes in a hot oven, 200°C/400°F/mark 6, before serving.

Suggested wines

Regaleali Bianco, Torbato (Italy); Graves Blanc (France); Californian Johannisberg Riesling (U.S.A.); Riesling (Australia).

Ravioli with sea bass

Preparation: 1 hour 20 minutes
(+2 hours to clean the
mussels)

600 g/1¼ lb ravioli
275 g/10 oz mussels
5 tbsp olive oil
1 clove garlic
1 large mushroom
1 tbsp chopped fresh parsley

2 tbsp single cream
1 tsp freshly made tomato
sauce
salt, black pepper

For the pasta
200 g/7 oz flour
4 tbsp white wine
1 egg
salt

For the filling
225 g/8 oz sea bass fillet
2 tbsp fresh breadcrumbs
6 tbsp milk
pinch marjoram
pinch nutmeg
1 tbsp grated Parmesan
1 egg yolk
4 tbsp single cream
salt, black pepper

1 Steam the fish for 8–10 minutes or until tender, then chop finely. Mix together with the breadcrumbs soaked in milk then squeezed out, marjoram, nutmeg, Parmesan, egg yolk, cream, salt and pepper.

2 Prepare and roll out a thin sheet of pasta (p. 180). Brush one half lightly with water and place small balls of filling at 4-cm/1½-in intervals.

3 Cover with the other half of pasta and press around the edges of the filling to seal. Cut out ravioli using a pastry wheel, then cook in plenty of boiling salted water for 5 minutes. Drain well and serve in individual dishes. Keep hot.

4 Place the well scrubbed mussels in a covered frying pan over high heat for 3 minutes until the shells open. Remove from their shells. Heat the olive oil in a frying pan, cut the garlic in half and brown lightly. Discard the garlic and add the finely diced mushroom and the chopped parsley. Heat for 2 minutes then add the chopped mussels, cream and tomato sauce. Season with salt and pepper, simmer for 3 minutes then pour the sauce over the ravioli.

Suggested wines

Pinot Bianco del Collio, Montecarlo Bianco (Italy); Montrachet (France); Californian Chardonnay (U.S.A.); Müller Thurgau (Germany).

Tagliolini with mullet à l'orange

Preparation: 1 hour

275 g/10 oz tagliolini
350 g/12 oz small red mullet
6 tbsp olive oil
salt
4 tbsp fresh orange juice
6 slices orange
½ clove garlic
black pepper

For the pasta
200 g/7 oz flour
2 eggs
salt

Suggested wines

Sauvignon del Collio, Sylvaner dell'Alto Adige (Italy);
Gewürztraminer d'Alsace (France); Californian
Johannisberg Riesling (U.S.A.); Rhine Riesling (Germany).

1 Bone the red mullet and divide into fillets.

2 Pour half the olive oil into a shallow ovenproof dish. Place the mullet in the oil and sprinkle with salt.

3 Pour the orange juice over the mullet, place the orange slices on top and transfer to a preheated oven, 180°C/350°F/mark 4, for 7 minutes.

4 Cook the tagliolini (p. 181) in boiling salted water for 3–4 minutes until *al dente*. Drain.

5 Heat the remaining oil in a large frying pan and lightly brown the sliced garlic.

6 Discard the garlic, add the drained tagliolini followed by the cooking juices from the mullet.

7 Serve the tagliolini in individual dishes sprinkled lightly with freshly ground black pepper and garnished with broken-up pieces of red mullet.

Spaghettini with sole

Preparation: 20 minutes (+2
    hours to marinate the sole)

225 g/8 oz spaghettini
275 g/10 oz sole fillet
salt
2 tbsp lemon juice
5 tbsp olive oil
2 ripe tomatoes

1 tsp diced onion
2 tbsp chopped fresh parsley
pinch chilli powder

1 Cut the sole into strips
8 mm × 3 cm/¼ × 1¼ in.

2 Place in a bowl, sprinkle with
salt, the lemon juice and 1 tbsp
olive oil and marinate for 2
hours.

3 Mix together in a bowl the
skinned, seeded and coarsely
chopped tomatoes, the onion,
parsley, chilli powder, a pinch
of salt and 1 tbsp oil. Mix well.

4 Cook the spaghettini in
plenty of boiling salted water
for 8–10 minutes until *al dente*.
Drain and leave under cold
running water for a few
minutes.

5 Warm the remaining oil in a
frying pan, remove from the
heat and add the drained
spaghettini. Stir to coat with oil.

6 Serve the spaghettini in
individual dishes, garnished
with the tomatoes, sole and a
little chopped parsley.

Suggested wines

Pinot Champenois dell'Oltrepò Pavese, Pinot Grigio
dell'Alto Adige (Italy); Champagne (France); Californian
Blanc de Blancs (U.S.A.); Rhine Sylvaner (Germany).

Tagliolini with jumbo prawns and artichokes

Preparation: 1 hour

275 g/10 oz tagliolini
2 medium artichokes
6 tbsp olive oil
salt
125 g/4 oz shelled jumbo
 prawns
½ tbsp chopped fresh parsley
black pepper

For the pasta
200 g/7 oz flour
2 eggs
salt

1 Discard any hard outer leaves and trim the sharp points of the remaining leaves of the artichokes. Cut in half, remove and discard the hairy choke and cut the artichokes into thin slices.

2 Heat 4 tbsp olive oil and the same quantity of water in a frying pan. Add the artichokes, sprinkle with salt, cover and simmer for 6 minutes.

3 Rinse the jumbo prawns and place on top of the artichokes. Sprinkle with salt, cover and cook over moderate heat for a further 5 minutes.

4 Cook the tagliolini (p. 181) in plenty of boiling salted water for 3–4 minutes until *al dente*. Drain.

5 Pour the tagliolini into the frying pan. Add the remaining oil, the parsley and a little black pepper. Mix carefully over high heat for 1 minute before serving.

Suggested wines

Torgiano Bianco, Vernaccia di San Gimignano (Italy); Bâtard Montrachet (France); Californian Gewürztraminer (U.S.A.); Rhine Riesling (Germany).

Ravioli with freshwater fish

Preparation: 1 hour 20 minutes

600 g/1¼ lb ravioli
salt
50 g/2 oz butter
6 fresh sage leaves

For the pasta
200 g/7 oz flour
2 eggs, salt

For the filling
225 g/8 oz freshwater fish fillets
   (trout, eel)
½ stick celery
1 sprig rosemary
175 g/6 oz spinach
salt, 1 egg
pinch thyme
25 g/1 oz butter
black pepper

1 Steam the fish or cook in 2.5 cm/1 in lightly salted water with the celery and rosemary for 4 minutes.

2 Cook the spinach in salted water for about 7 minutes. Drain well.

3 Flake the fish and finely chop the spinach.

4 Mix together in a bowl the flaked fish, spinach, egg, thyme, melted butter, salt and freshly ground black pepper and stir until smooth and well blended.

5 Prepare and roll out a sheet of pasta (p. 180). Brush half lightly with water and place small balls of filling at 4-cm/ 1½-in intervals. Cover with the second half of pasta and press round the edges of the filling to seal.

6 Cut out ravioli using a pastry wheel and cook in boiling salted water for 5 minutes. Drain and serve with sage-flavoured melted butter.

Suggested wines

Soave, Torgiano Bianco (Italy); Graves Blanc (France); Californian Chardonnay (U.S.A.); Rhine Sylvaner (Germany).

Spaghettini with sea urchins

Preparation: 40 minutes

225 g/8 oz spaghettini
24 sea urchins
salt
175 ml/6 fl oz olive oil
1 clove garlic
1 tsp chopped fresh parsley
black pepper

1 Put the sea urchins in a saucepan of boiling water for a few minutes. Drain and cut the sea urchins in half.

2 Cook the spaghettini in plenty of boiling salted water for 8–10 minutes until *al dente*. Drain under cold running water for 1 minute.

3 Heat half the olive oil in a large frying pan and brown half the finely diced garlic over low heat for 30 seconds. Discard the garlic.

4 Pour the spaghettini into the frying pan and turn to coat with the oil, adding the chopped parsley and freshly ground black pepper. Serve in individual dishes.

5 Place a few sea urchins on top of each serving.

6 Heat the remaining oil and garlic over low heat for 2 minutes. Strain and pour the oil over the sea urchins. Sprinkle lightly with pepper before serving.

This dish can be served hot if preferred. Do not cool the spaghettini and hold the frying pan over heat while turning them in the oil.

Suggested wines

Pinot Champenois di Franciacorta, Gavi (Italy); Champagne (France); Californian Blanc de Blancs (U.S.A.); Müller Thurgau (Germany).

PASTA SHAPES

Spaghetti, Bombolotti, Tortijoni,
Schiaffoni, Picchiettini, Pappardelle,
Fresine, Bucatini, Recchietelle,
Fusilli, Millerighe, Farfalloni,

Zitoni, Spaghettini, Canneroni,
Lasagne, Strozzapreti, Reginelle,
Bavette, Tajolini, Tajatelle,
Occhi de lupo, Zita, Lumaconi,

Pippe, Cazzetti d'angelo, Fischiotti,
Creste de Gallo, Maniche, Ditali,
Linguine, Rigatoni, Manicotti,
Corna de bue, Cornetti, Cornacopie.

Every region boasts its own shapes
and each prefers its own.

(Aldo Fabrizi, *La pastasciutta*)

DRIED PASTA

Spaghetti

Trenette

Pasta spirals

Spaghettini

Wholewheat spaghetti

Smooth macaroni

Smooth penne

Pizzoccheri

Pasta shells

Fluted maccheroncini

Fluted penne

ed wholewheat macaroni

Bucatini

Pasta
spirals

Smooth penne

Pasta bows

Pasta wheels

Orecchiette

Rigatoni

Fluted macaroni

Ditalini

Sardinian gnocchetti

Smooth maccheroncini

FRESH PASTA

Tortelloni

Pappardelle

Lasagne

Cannelloni

Cappelletti

Tortellini

Pansooti

Maltagliati

Tagliatelle

Tagliolini

Ravioli

How to cook pasta

The first and most important rule is to cook pasta in plenty of water — at least 1 litre/1¾ pints for every 125 g/4 oz pasta — in a large saucepan.

Add 1 dessertspoon of salt to every 1 litre/1¾ pints water.

Pour the pasta into the water when it begins to boil. Only filled pasta (ravioli, tortellini, etc.) is added just before the water reaches boiling point to avoid them bursting open.

When cooking fresh pasta or lasagne add 1–2 tablespoons of olive oil to the water to prevent the pasta sticking together.

Stir the pasta as soon as you pour it into the saucepan, then stir frequently during cooking.

For the best results (and evenly cooked pasta) the water should boil neither too vigorously nor too slowly, but over moderate heat. This is particularly important for fresh and filled pasta.

Do not cover the saucepan while the pasta is cooking.

Drain the pasta when it is *al dente* (tender but still with a little 'bite'). Remember that it will continue to cook for a couple of minutes after it is turned into the colander.

Filled pasta, gnocchi and freshly made lasagne should be lifted out of the water with a large slotted spoon or ladle as soon as they rise to the surface. Dried pasta and less fragile fresh pasta can be poured straight into the colander.

Drain the pasta well if you are serving it straight into individual dishes. Leave a little of the cooking water with it if you are dressing it with a sauce in a large serving tureen or if it is returned to the frying pan for a few minutes.

If you want to keep cooked pasta for later use, drain it when it is *al dente* and submerge in cold water for at least three minutes to stop further cooking. To reheat it, plunge it into boiling water for a couple of minutes, then drain well.

The classic way to cook spaghetti is to keep it whole and not break it into shorter lengths. Place the spaghetti in the boiling water and push slowly as the pasta softens until it is completely submerged. Stir immediately.

For perfect success it is important to match the right kind of pasta with the most suitable sauce. As a general rule fresh pasta marries well with lighter, more delicate flavours, such as sauces made with spinach, butter, cream, prosciutto, mushrooms or tomatoes. Dried pasta is better suited to more pronounced flavours and more piquant ingredients, such as garlic, chilli pepper, game, pork and the richer meat sauces.

Sauces

As well as the sauces contained in the recipes the following can be used to accompany a variety of pasta dishes.

Creamed pepper sauce

2 sweet peppers
150 ml/5 fl oz light cream
salt

Place the sweet peppers in a hot oven, 200°C/400°F/mark 6, or under the grill until the skins blister and can be rubbed off. Skin the peppers and discard the seeds. Cut into small pieces and place in a blender or food processor with the cream and a pinch of salt. Blend until smooth; transfer to a small saucepan or frying pan, and cook for 5 minutes, stirring with a whisk.

Pesto sauce

25 g/1 oz pine nuts
50 g/2 oz fresh basil leaves
salt
2 cloves garlic
1 tbsp grated Parmesan
1 tbsp grated Pecorino cheese
200 ml/7 fl oz olive oil

Lightly toast the pine nuts in a hot oven, 200°C/400°F/mark 6. Rinse and dry the basil leaves. Place in a mortar or blender, add salt, garlic and the pine nuts and pound or blend to a paste. Add the cheeses gradually. When the paste is smooth, transfer to a bowl and gradually stir in the olive oil using a wooden spoon.

Tomato sauce

450 g/1 lb ripe tomatoes
salt
3 tbsp olive oil
1 tbsp chopped fresh basil

Skin the tomatoes (cover them with boiling water for a few minutes to loosen the skin), remove the seeds and chop the flesh into small pieces. Place in a frying pan with salt to taste and 1 tbsp olive oil and cook for 6 minutes. Sieve the cooked tomatoes. Pour the sauce back into the frying pan, add the remaining oil and the basil and cook for 1 minute.

Meat sauce

15 g/½ oz butter
275 g/10 oz ground beef
50 g/2 oz fresh spicy sausage
1 bay leaf
½ onion
1 clove
salt
225 g/8 oz tomatoes

Melt the butter in a heavy saucepan; add the ground beef, crumbled sausage, bay leaf and the ½ onion stuck with a clove, and cook over low heat for 20 minutes, stirring frequently. Add salt and the skinned, seeded and chopped tomatoes; bring to the boil and simmer for about 1 hour, adding a little stock or warm water and 1 tsp meat extract if the sauce becomes too dry. Cook for a further 20 minutes then remove the onion and bay leaf.

Mock meat sauce

1 onion
1 stick celery
1 carrot
1 tbsp olive oil
50 g/2 oz fatty prosciutto
250 ml/9 fl oz white wine
350 g/12 oz tomatoes
salt
pepper
1 tbsp chopped fresh parsley and marjoram

Finely chop the onion, celery and carrot. Heat the olive oil in a frying pan and brown the chopped vegetables and finely sliced prosciutto. Add the wine, heat for 2 minutes then add the chopped tomatoes. Season with salt and pepper and cook over medium heat for about 45 minutes.

Caper sauce

2 tbsp capers
1 clove garlic
1 tbsp anchovy paste
250 ml/9 fl oz olive oil
juice of ½ lemon

Pound the capers and garlic or blend in a food processor. Place in a bowl and mix in the anchovy paste. Stir in the olive oil gradually, followed by the lemon juice and mix until well blended.

Mornay sauce

100 g/3½ oz butter
30 g/1 oz flour
250 ml/9 fl oz milk
salt
50 g/2 oz grated Parmesan

Make a white sauce: melt 40 g/1½ oz butter in a small saucepan, add the flour and stir over heat for 1 minute. Gradually stir in the hot milk, waiting for the sauce to thicken after each addition. Add salt to taste, then simmer for about 10 minutes. Add the remaining butter, cut into pieces, and the grated Parmesan and mix well.

How to prepare home-made pasta

FRESH PASTA

Sift the flour into a heap on a work surface or marble top and make a well in the centre (1). Pour the whole eggs one at a time (1 egg for every 100 g/ 3½ oz flour) into the well (2), add salt and beat in the eggs with a fork. Continue to beat with a fork (3) until the mixture can be worked by hand. Knead the dough for about 10 minutes by hand (4). When the dough is smooth and elastic roll out on a floured work surface to the desired thickness (5).

1 person

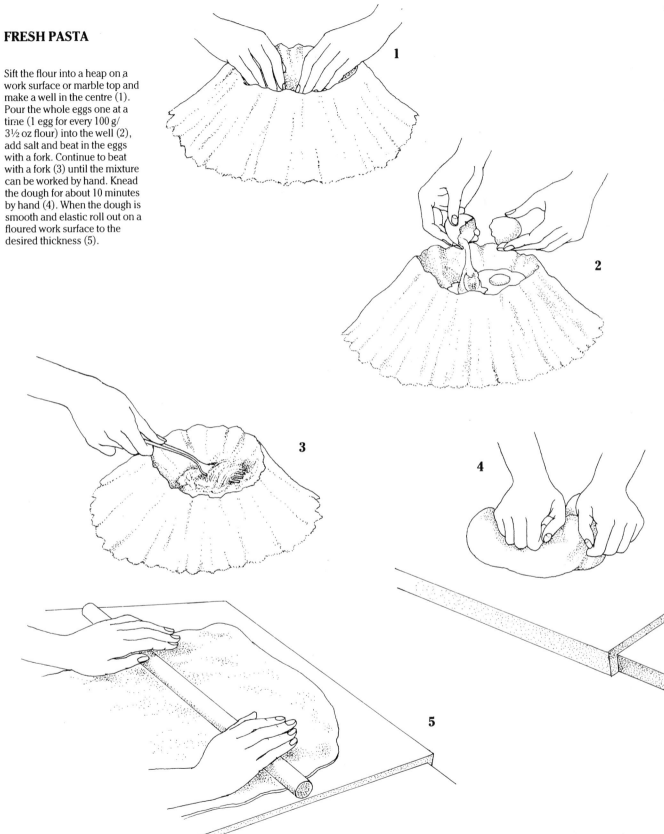

Fresh spinach pasta

Use 100 g/3½ oz spinach for every 100 g/3½ oz flour. Cook the spinach in the minimum of boiling salted water for 5–10 minutes or until tender. Drain well and blend in a liquidizer (1–2). Pour into the well in the centre after the beaten eggs (3). Mix together and knead as illustrated opposite.

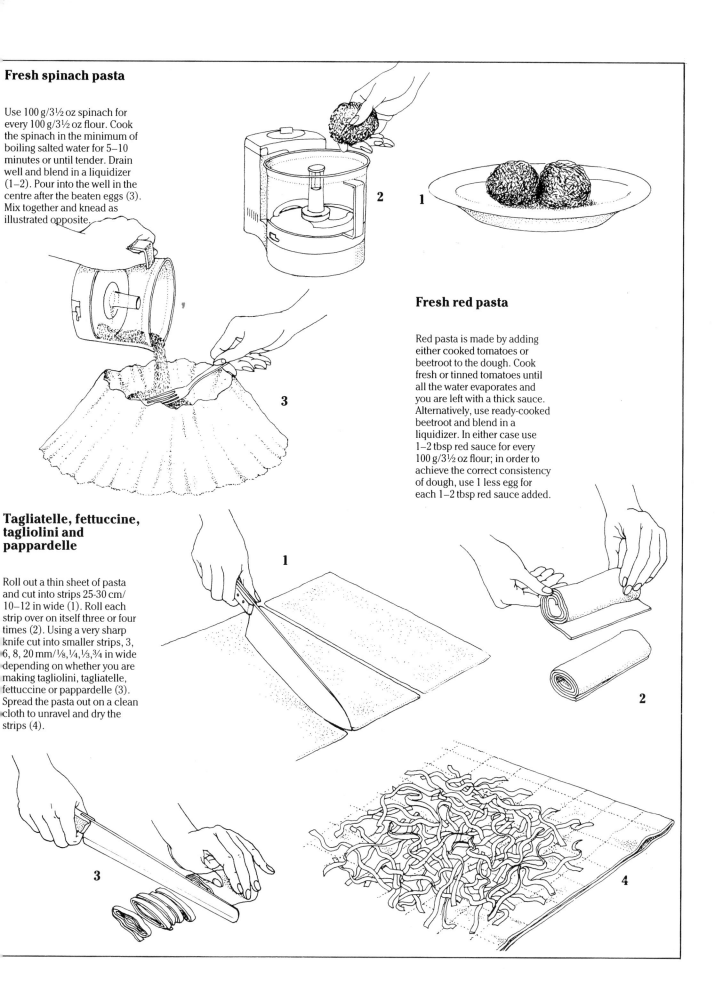

Fresh red pasta

Red pasta is made by adding either cooked tomatoes or beetroot to the dough. Cook fresh or tinned tomatoes until all the water evaporates and you are left with a thick sauce. Alternatively, use ready-cooked beetroot and blend in a liquidizer. In either case use 1–2 tbsp red sauce for every 100 g/3½ oz flour; in order to achieve the correct consistency of dough, use 1 less egg for each 1–2 tbsp red sauce added.

Tagliatelle, fettuccine, tagliolini and pappardelle

Roll out a thin sheet of pasta and cut into strips 25-30 cm/ 10–12 in wide (1). Roll each strip over on itself three or four times (2). Using a very sharp knife cut into smaller strips, 3, 6, 8, 20 mm/⅛,¼,⅓,¾ in wide depending on whether you are making tagliolini, tagliatelle, fettuccine or pappardelle (3). Spread the pasta out on a clean cloth to unravel and dry the strips (4).

Lasagne

To make squares of lasagne, roll out a sheet of pasta and cut into 12-cm/5-in squares (1). Place the lasagne one at a time in a large saucepan of boiling salted water (2) with 1 tbsp olive oil to prevent them sticking. Cook for 3–5 minutes; drain when *al dente* (3) and spread out to dry on a clean cloth. Place a layer of lasagne in the bottom of a buttered ovenproof baking dish (4). Cover with the filling (5) and continue layering with pasta and filling until all the ingredients are used up. Finish with a layer of pasta and place a few flakes of butter on top. For spinach lasagne, see instructions for 'Fresh spinach pasta,' p.181.

Cannelloni

Proceed as for lasagne as far as step 3. Place a spoonful of filling in the centre of each square of pasta (1). Roll up into cannelloni (2). Arrange in a buttered ovenproof baking dish and cover with sauce.

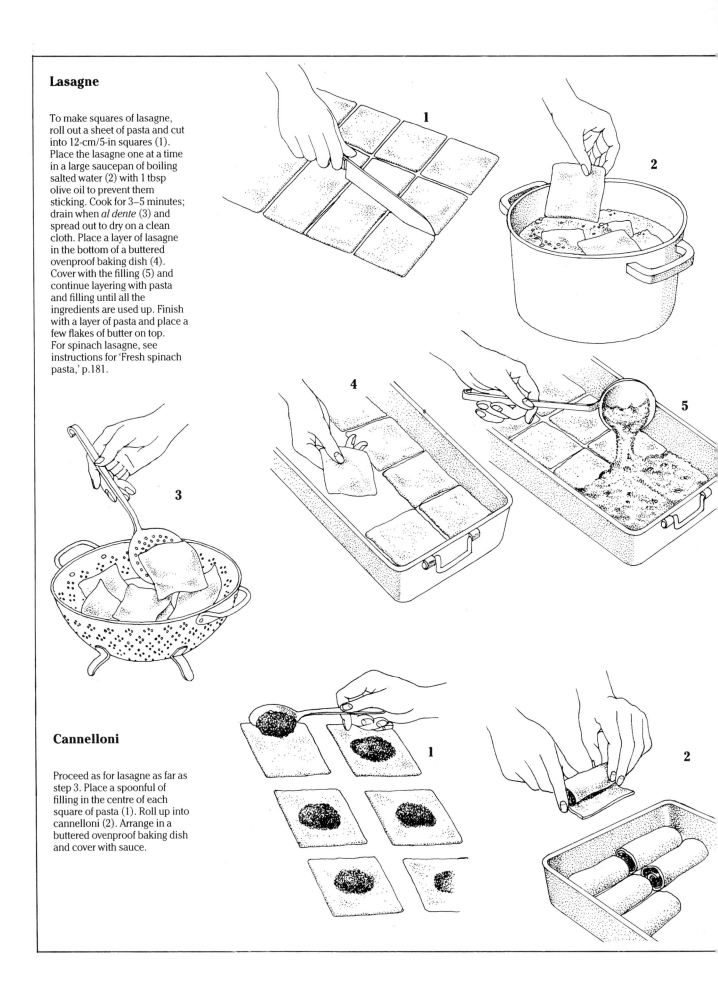

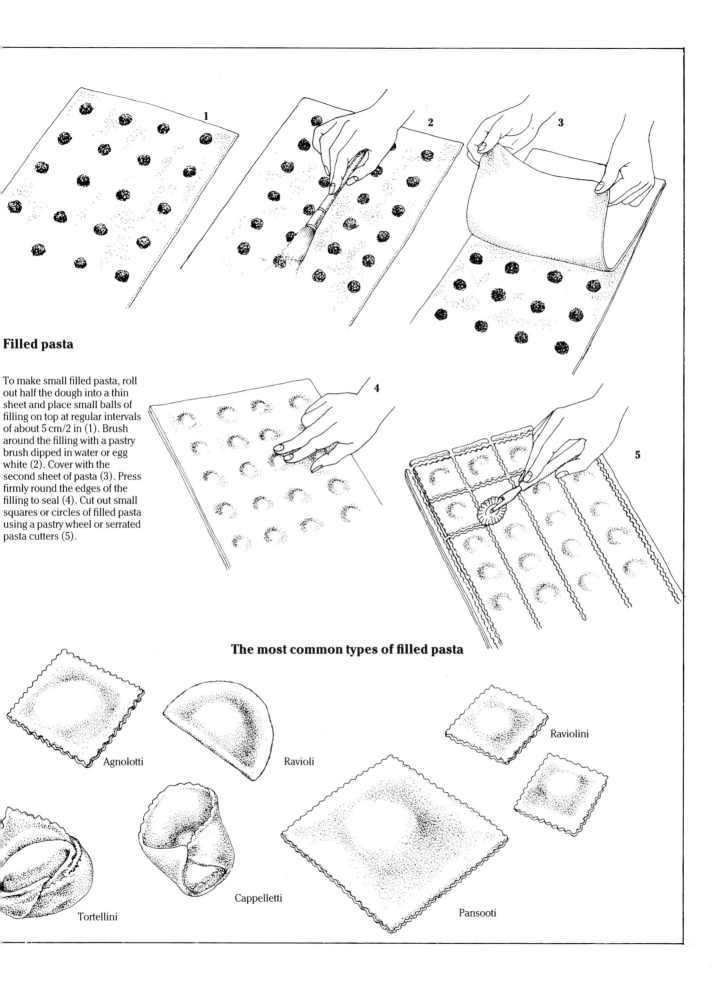

Filled pasta

To make small filled pasta, roll out half the dough into a thin sheet and place small balls of filling on top at regular intervals of about 5 cm/2 in (1). Brush around the filling with a pastry brush dipped in water or egg white (2). Cover with the second sheet of pasta (3). Press firmly round the edges of the filling to seal (4). Cut out small squares or circles of filled pasta using a pastry wheel or serrated pasta cutters (5).

The most common types of filled pasta

Agnolotti

Ravioli

Raviolini

Tortellini

Cappelletti

Pansooti

SPECIAL TYPES OF PASTA

Orecchiette

Sift the flour and an equal amount of fine semolina into a heap on a work surface and make a well in the centre. Pour in a little warm salted water and knead until firm and elastic. Roll into long sausages 2 cm/¾ in in diameter(1). Cut into circles 3 mm/⅛ in thick (2). Press in the middle of each circle using a knife with a rounded tip, then push into the shape of a little hat using your thumb (3). Leave to stand for at least a day before using.

Bigoli

Make the dough using equal parts flour and fine semolina, eggs (1 for every 150 g/5 oz floury ingredients), a little water and a pinch of salt. Push the dough through a pasta-making machine or hand grinder (1–2), using a disc with 5-mm/¼-in holes. Leave the bigoli to dry on a clean cloth (3).

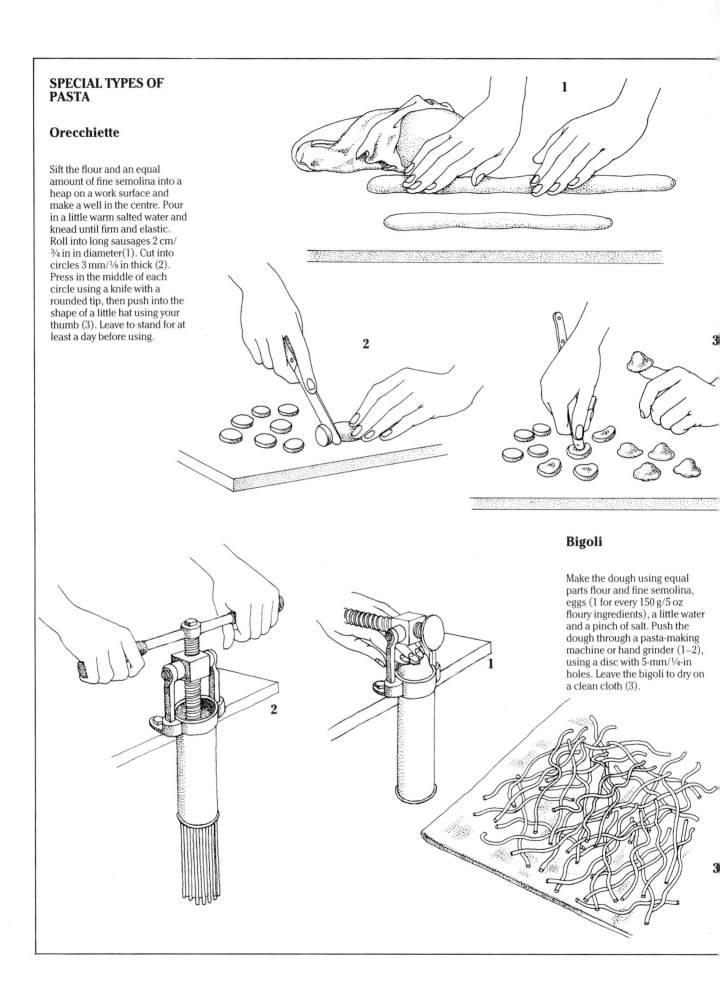

Crespelle (crêpes)

Beat together in a bowl 100 g/ 3½ oz flour, 2 eggs, 1 tbsp melted butter and a pinch of salt. Gradually add 200 ml/ 7 fl oz milk, beating constantly until well blended (1). Lightly butter a non-stick 20-cm/8-in frying pan. Place over moderate heat and when hot add enough batter to cover the base thinly (2). As soon as the batter sets, turn carefully and quickly cook the other side (3).

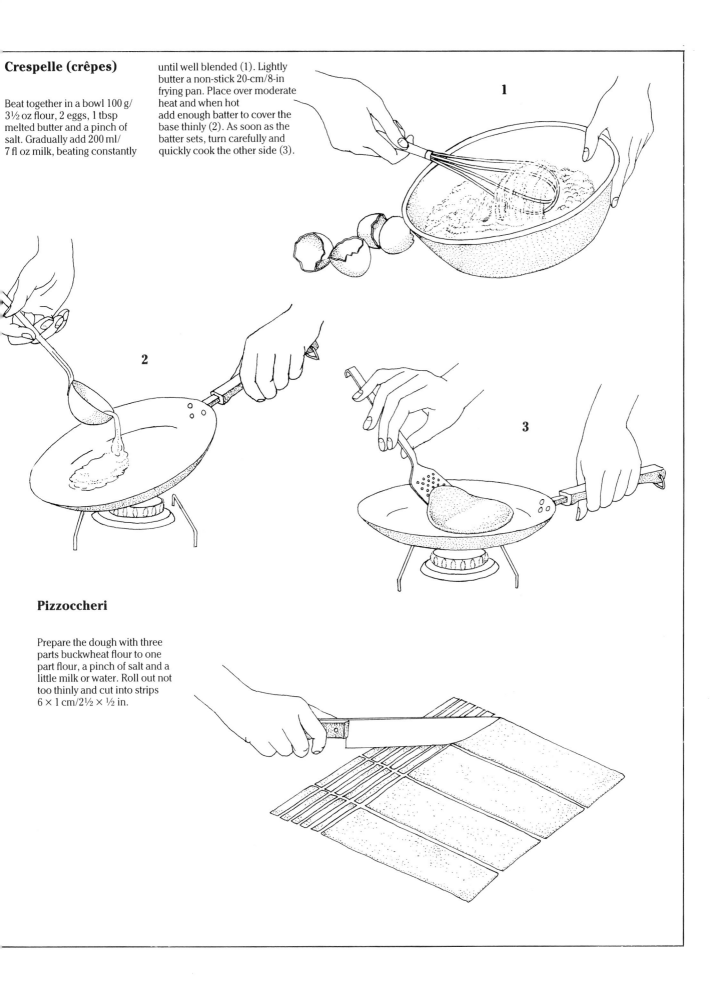

Pizzoccheri

Prepare the dough with three parts buckwheat flour to one part flour, a pinch of salt and a little milk or water. Roll out not too thinly and cut into strips 6 × 1 cm/2½ × ½ in.

Garganelli

Prepare a dough with two parts flour to one part fine semolina. Add 1 egg for every 100 g/3½ oz floury ingredients, a pinch of nutmeg and salt and a little grated Parmesan. Roll out into a sheet and cut into 7-cm/3-in squares (1). Roll the squares of pasta diagonally around a thin wooden spoon handle, pressing firmly so that the pasta sticks (2–3). To create a ridged effect for garganelli or macaroni roll each one over a ridged wooden block (4). Slide the garganelli off the wooden handle and leave to dry (5).

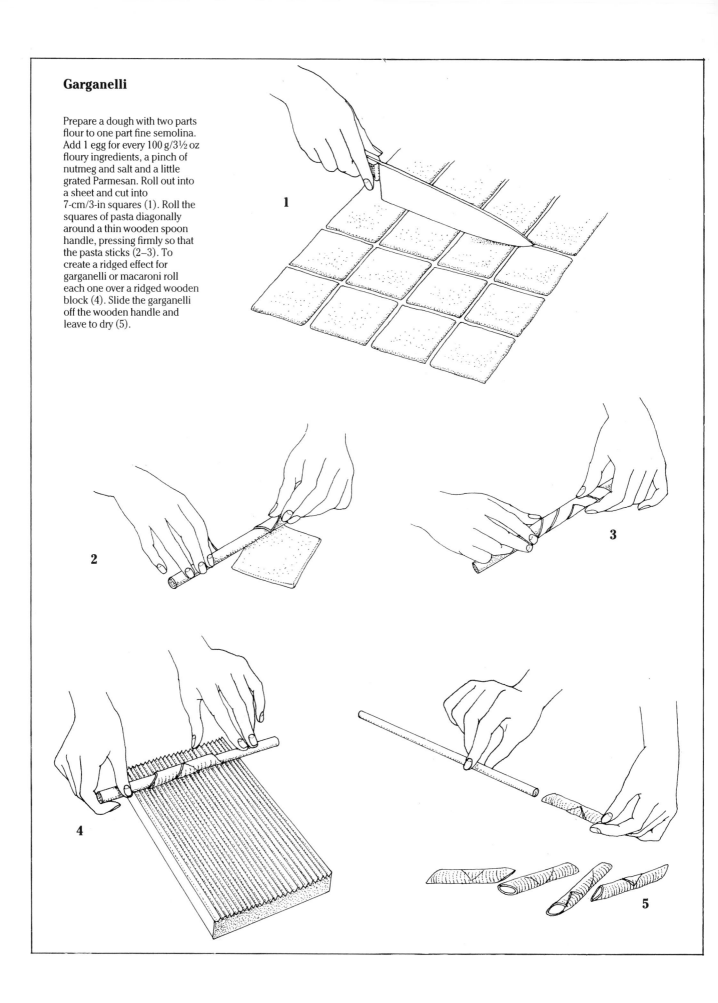

Glossary

Cremona Mustard *Mostarda di frutta*, a speciality of Cremona, is a sweet fruit pickle consisting of whole fruits preserved in sugar syrup flavoured with mustard oil. The whole fruits used may include pears, plums, figs, apricots, melon, pumpkin, cherries, etc. The combination of sweet and sour makes this an excellent accompaniment to cold meats.

Mascarpone This delicately-flavoured fresh cheese has a high fat content and is often combined with sweet ingredients for desserts and with savoury ingredients for pasta dishes. If unobtainable, substitute any brand of unflavoured cream cheese.

Mortadella A speciality of Bologna, mortadella is a mild sausage, usually made of pork and flavoured with garlic, coriander and white wine. Serve very thinly sliced.

Pancetta Made from the belly of the pig, this hard fatty bacon is either salted or smoked and is frequently used in the preparation of sauces. If unobtainable, substitute smoked fatty bacon.

Porcini These mushrooms, also known as 'ceps' or 'cèpes', are the most widely used in Italy. They are collected in vast quantities in the autumn and are available dried all year round. Dried mushrooms should be soaked for 20–30 min, then drained and squeezed before use.

Prosciutto The most well-known prosciutto is perhaps the cured ham from Parma which is usually sliced wafer-thin and served as an antipasto.

Radicchio or red Treviso chicory is often served grilled in the Veneto and is also used in certain types of filled pasta. Most commonly used as a salad vegetable.

Ricotta marzotica This dried ricotta, originally produced in Apulia, is aged for several months and used for grating. If unavailable, substitute Pecorino or Parmesan.

Sea date (*datteri di mare*) Shellfish in the shape of a date stone, found off the coast of Genoa and used in fish stews. If unavailable, substitute mussels or other molluscs.

Utensils

Index